Maria Nye Buell

Centennial Cookery Book

Maria Nye Buell

Centennial Cookery Book

ISBN/EAN: 9783744790062

Printed in Europe, USA, Canada, Australia, Japan

Cover: Foto ©Lupo / pixelio.de

More available books at **www.hansebooks.com**

TX
715
.B942

STANDARD HOUSEHOLD REMEDIES!

DR. D. JAYNE'S
FAMILY MEDICINES.

Are prepared with great care, expressly for Family use, and are so admirably calculated to preserve health and remove disease that no family should be without them. They consist of

JAYNE'S EXPECTORANT, for Colds, Coughs, Asthma, Consumption, and all Pulmonary and Bronchial Affections. It promotes expectoration and allays inflammation.

JAYNE'S TONIC VERMIFUGE, for Worms, Dyspepsia, Piles, General Debility, &c. An excellent Tonic for Children, and a beneficial remedy in many of the ailments of the young.

JAYNE'S CARMINATIVE BALSAM, for Bowel and Summer Complaints, Colics, Cramp, Cholera, &c. A certain cure for Diarrhœa, Cholera Morbus, and Inflammation of the Bowels.

JAYNE'S ALTERATIVE, of established efficacy in Purifying the Blood, and for curing Scrofula, Goitre Dropsy, Salt Rheum, Epilepsy, Cancers, and Disease of the Skin and Bones.

JAYNE'S LINIMENT OR COUNTER-IRRITANT, for Sprains Bruises, Soreness in the Bones and Muscles, Rheumatism, and usefu in all cases where an external application is required.

JAYNE'S SANATIVE PILLS, a valuable Purgative and a certain cure for all Bilious Affections, Liver Complaints, Costiveness, Dyspepsia, and Sick Headache.

JAYNE'S HAIR TONIC, for the Preservation, Beauty, Growth and Restoration of the Hair. A pleasant dressing for the hair, and a useful toilet article.

JAYNE'S SPECIFIC FOR TAPE WORM, a certain, safe and prompt remedy.

In settlements and localities where the attendance of a Physician cannot be readily obtained, Families will find these Remedies of great service. The Directions which accompany them are in plain, unprofessional language, easily understood by all and, in addition, Jayne's Medical Almanac and Guide to Health, to be had gratis of all Agents, contains, besides a reliable Calendar, a Catalogue of Diseases, THE SYMPTOMS BY WHICH THEY MAY BE KNOWN, *together with advice as to the proper remedies to be used.*

All of   are sold by Druggists gener

When

You are offered a Paint, and informed by a dealer that it is just as good as the Longman & Martinez Paint, buy it quick; provided that the dealer is responsible and willing to give you a signed guarantee, in as strong and forcible language as the one which is attached to every gallon of the L. & M. Pure Prepared Paints sold only by W. H. Buell & Co., Marietta, O.

THE MARIETTA BOOK STORE.

E. R. ALDERMAN & SONS, Proprietors.

C. E. GLINES, Manager.

CARRIES THE LARGEST LINE OF
  MISCELLANEOUS BOOKS, TEXT BOOKS,
    CHILDREN'S ILLUSTRATED BOOKS,
      FINE STATIONERY, ETC.,
          OF ANY HOUSE IN THE CITY
HEADQUARTERS FOR ARTISTS' GOODS AND ARTISTS' SUPPLIES.
  FINE LINES OF PICTURES AND PICTURE FRAMES.
    A FULL LINE OF SMALL MUSICAL GOODS
         AND PIANOS AND ORGANS.
AGENTS FOR KNABE, EVERETT, HOWARD AND OTHER PIANOS,
    CLOUGH AND WARREN AND THE CHURCH ORGAN.
    GOOD GOODS, CLOSE MARGINS, CASH PAYMENTS.

REGISTER BUILDING,   MARIETTA, O.

A. J. Richards,

The Druggist,

27 Greene St.,

   *Marietta, O.*

KINGSFORD'S OSWEGO STARCH

THE BEST IN THE WORLD.
QUALITY ALWAYS UNIFORM.

THE
NEW WRAPPERS MAKING MOST ATTRACTIVE SHELF GOODS.

KINGSFORD'S CORN STARCH

FOR THE TABLE,

IS MOST DELICIOUS FOR PUDDINGS,
BLANC MANGE, CUSTARDS, ETC.

AND IS PERFECTLY PURE.

To Secure the Best — the Unadulterated Article See that the Name

T. KINGSFORD & SON, OSWEGO, N. Y.

Is on every Box and every Package.

VALENTINE'S MEAT-JUICE
ESTABLISHED 1871 BY
MANN S. VALENTINE,
RICHMOND, VIRGINIA, U. S. A.

REPORT OF THE JUDGES OF THE CENTENNIAL EXPOSITION.

"*For excellence of the method of its preparation, whereby it more nearly represents fresh meat than any other extract of meat, its freedom from disagreeable taste, its fitness for immediate absorption, and the perfection in which it retains its good qualities in warm climates.*"

TESTIMONIALS.

New York — J. MARION SIMS, M. D. — I prescribe VALENTINE'S MEAT-JUICE daily, and like it better than any preparation of the sort I have ever used.

Philadelphia — D. HAYES AGNEW, M. D. — I have been using for some time the MEAT-JUICE prepared by Mr. Valentine, and I think with excellent results.

PLYMPTON, ENGLAND, January 25, 1887.

VALENTINE'S MEAT-JUICE is excellent; and, I believe, superior to any similar preparations of the kind now in use. It will, when administered in cold water, be relished and retained by the most irritable stomach, when every other kind of food is loathed. I shall not fail to use and recommend it.

J. M. MINTER, M. D., *F. R. C. S.;*

[*Dr. Minter is Hon. Phys. to H. M. the Queen, and Sur'g. Ext. to H. R. H. the Prince of Wales.*]

[Translated from the German]

BERLIN, GERMANY. December 24, 1878.

The aqueous solution prepared with VALENTINE'S MEAT-JUICE has an agreeable taste, and it acts both, according to its composition and the experiments made by ourselves with convalescents and delicate persons, as an easily-digested and life-giving remedy.

DR. OSCAR LEIBREICH,

Ord: Professor of Materia Medica in the University of Berlin, and Director of the Pharmacological Institute.

DR. RUDOLF VIRCHOW,

Ord: Professor of Pathology, Director of the Pathological Institute in the University.

VALENTINES MEAT-JUICE
CAN BE PURCHASED OF DRUGGISTS EVERYWHERE

☞ A cyclone is the nearest approach to Dead Shot in its destructive power. It makes a clean sweep.

WHAT TO EAT?

And How to Cook it, is Most Fully and Accurately Set Forth in This Book.

WHAT TO WEAR?

And Where to Get it, and How to Make it, are Questions Not Less Important.

S. R. TURNER & CO.

The Largest and Leading Dry Goods Firm in Marietta Will Help You Answer these Questions, Showing You an Exceedingly Large and Varied Stock of All Kinds of Goods Pertaining to the DRY GOODS TRADE, and Furnishing the Fashion Sheets and Other Publications of the Butterick Publishing Co., as a Help in Choice of Styles. The Butterick Patterns, of Which they Keep a Full Stock, are generally Conceded to be the Most Reliable and Perfect Patterns Published.

☞ The invasion of your peaceful couch by a horde of bloodthirsty savages, may be easily prevented and the enemy utterly destroyed by the use of *Dutcher's Dead Shot*.

SHORT HINTS
ON
SOCIAL ETIQUETTE.

Compiled from the Latest and Best Works on the Subject by "Aunt Matilda."

PRICE 40 CENTS.

THIS book should be in every family desirous of knowing "the proper thing to do." We all desire to behave properly and to know what is the best school of manners. What shall we teach our children, that they may go out into the world well bred men and women?

"**Short Hints**" contains the answer and will be mailed to any address, postage prepaid on receipt of price.

SPECIAL

Until further notice we will mail each of our friends a copy of the above valuable book gratis and free of postage, if they will mail us 15 wrappers of Dobbins' Electric Soap.

By folding up the wrappers as you would a newspaper, the postage will only be 2 cts.

Always put your full name and address on the outside of the bundle and write the word 'Etiquette' also, and then we will know who sends it.

I. L. CRAGIN & CO.,
PHILADELPHIA, PA.

The Oldest Drug House
in Washington Co.

WELL AND FAVORABLY KNOWN THROUGHOUT THE SURROUNDING COUNTRY, AS THE MOST RELIABLE PLACE FOR

Pure Drugs, Medicines,

Finst Spices and Best Baking Powder.

We manufacture our own Baking Powder of only the purest materials. Contains absolutely no adulterations, and costs from 10 to 20 cents per pound less than other first-class Baking Powders.

Headquarters for all kinds of Paints and Oils, French and American Window Glass, Figured and Colored Glass, Wall Paper and Window Curtains.

Agents for *Granite Floor Paint* and *Neil's Ready-Mixed Carriage Paints.*

We have the best equipped Prescription Department in this section, and great care is exercised in preparing Physicians' Prescriptions.

W. H. Buell & Co.

WHOLESALE AND RETAIL DRUGGISTS,

No. 22 Front Street,   Marietta, O.

PIONEER DRUG STORE.

Health and Vigor for the Brain and
Nervous System!

Crosby's Vitalized Phos-phites

Composed of the Nerve-giving Principles of the
Ox-Brain and the Embryo of the Wheat
and Oat.

THIS is a standard preparation with all physicians who treat mental or nervous disorders. The formula is on every label.
Its chemical composition is superintended by a Professor of Chemistry.

As it is identical in its composition with brain-matter, it is rapidly absorbed, and quickly relieves the depression from intellectual efforts, fatigue, loss of memory, or mental irritability. Sleeplessness, irritation, nervous exhaustion, inability to work or study, is but a **brain-hunger** — in urgent cases, **brain-starvation**. This brain nutriment quickly feeds the hungry nerves and restores brain-power. It is a cure for nervous disorders and debility. It aids in the growth of the brain, the bones, the teeth, the skin, and nails of children. It directly aids a child to learn.

BRAIN WORKERS NEED BRAIN FOOD.

F. CROSBY & CO. 56 WEST 25TH ST. NEW YORK.

For Sale by Druggists; or by Mail in P. O. Order, Bill or Postage Stamps, $1.

1 POUND CAN	KENTON	RETAILS FOR 20c.
1-2 POUND CAN	BAKING	RETAILS FOR 10c.
1-2 POUND CAN	POWDER	RETAILS FOR 10c.

N. B. In regard to this POWDER we have to say, there is no better made. It has few equals and no superior. We do not except other brands because they may cost more money. While the price of KENTON is much less than some, it is equal to the most costly in quality. Buy KENTON POWDER and you will not only save money, but have light, sweet and wholesome bread.

MANUFACTURED ONLY BY

POTTER, PARLIN & CO. CINCINNATI, O.

FOR SALE BY ALL GROCERS.

ELECTRIC BRUSHES ETC.

DR. SCOTT'S
ELECTRIC CORSETS AND BELTS.

| Corsets, $1.00, 1.50, 2.00, 3.00. | Belts, (Ladies' or Gents'.) $3.00. | Nursing Corset. Price $1.50. | Abdominal Corset. Price $3.00. |

Our Corsets Are Double Stitched And Will Not Rip.

If you have any pain, ache, or ill-feeling from any cause, if you seem "pretty well," yet lack energy and do not "feel up to the mark," if you suffer from disease, we beg you to at once try these remarkable curatives. They cannot and do not injure like medicine.

Always doing good, never harm. There is no shock or sensation felt in wearing them. There is no waiting a long time for results; electro-magnetism acts quickly; generally the first week, more frequently the first day, and often even during the first hour they are worn their wonderful curative powers are felt.

The mind becomes active, the nerves and sluggish circulation are stimulated, and all the old-time health and good feeling come back. They are constructed on scientific principles imparting an exhilerating, health-giving current to the whole system. Professional men assert that there is hardly a disease which Electricity or Magnetism may not benefit or cure, and they daily practice the same, as your own physician will inform you.

The prices are as follows: $1, $1.50, $2 and $3 for the Corsets and $3 each for the Belts. The accompanying cut represents our No. 2 or $1.50 Corset. We have also a beautiful French-shaped Sateen Corset at $3; a Sateen Abdominal Corset, and a short Sateen Corset at $2. The $1 and $1.50 goods are made of fine Japan, elegant in shape, strong and durable. Nursing Corsets, $1.50; Misses', 75c. All are double stitched. We have a fine linen netting Ventilating Corset at $1.50. We make all the above from 18 to 30 inches. The Abdominal only are made as large as 38. Gent's and Ladies' Belts $3 each; Ladies' Abdominal Supporter, an invaluable article, $12. We make all these Corsets in dove and white only. They are sent out in a handsome box, accompanied by a silver-plated compass, by which the Electro-Magnetic influence can be tested. We will send either kind to any address, postpaid, on receipt of price, with 20 cents added for packing or registration; and we guarantee safe delivery into your hands. Remit in Post-office Money-order, Draft, Check, or in currency by Registered Letter at our risk. In ordering, kindly mention THIS BOOK and state exact size of corset usually worn. Make all remittances payable to GEO. A. SCOTT, 842 BROADWAY, NEW YORK.

N. B.—Each Corset is stamped with the English coat-of-arms, and the name of the Proprietors, THE PALL MALL ELECTRIC ASSOCIATION.

Send for pamphlet of other appliances adapted to all parts of the body.

A GREAT SUCCESS.

☞ A Good, Live Canvassing Agent WANTED in your town for these splendidly advertised and best selling goods in the market. LIBERAL PAY, QUICK SALES. Satisfaction Guaranteed. Apply at once. GEO. A. SCOTT, 842 BROADWAY, N. Y.

CENTENNIAL
Cookery Book.

SOLD FOR THE BENEFIT OF

THE WOMAN'S CENTENNIAL ASSOCIATION

OF MARIETTA, OHIO.

"I crack my brains to find out tempting sauces."

"Cook, see all your sauces
Be sharp and poynant in the palate, that they may
Commend you; look to your roast and baked meats handsomely,
And what new kickshaws and delicate made things."
Beaumont and Fletcher.

1788.   APRIL 7.   1888.

TIMES PRINT, MARIETTA, O.
1887.

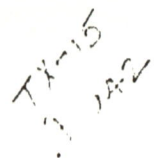

"We may live without poetry, music, and art;
We may live without conscience, and live without heart;
We may live without friends; we may live without books;
But civilized man cannot live without cooks."
Lord Lytton.

———

"The turnpike road to people's hearts I find
Lies through their mouths, or I mistake mankind."
Peter Pindar.

———

"I own that nothing like good chew succeeds."

———

"When dinner has opprest one,
I think it is perhaps the gloomiest hour
Which turns up out of the sad twenty-four.
Byron.

COPYRIGHT, 1887,
BY WOMAN'S CENTENNIAL ASSOCIATION,
MARIETTA, OHIO.

Preface.

Of making Cook Books there is no end, and it may be granted that they are similar. Yet it is believed this book will be valuable to any one, as its contents were gathered by competent persons from a large number of most experienced housewives, and the receipes are such, as have been thoroughly tried and approved.

An effort has been made to preserve some of the methods of our grandmothers which have fallen into disuse, under change of circumstances, but which are remembered to have produced most excellent results for the palate.

Few persons now care to prepare the Pickled Beef, Ham and Pork, the Rye and Indian Bread, the pounded Biscuit and Crackers, the Home brewed Beer of the early part of the century, but to those who remember these things they have never been surpassed for goodness, and there is a suspicion that like the great Artist's colors the old recipes were "mixed with brains."

In this day of tracing pedigrees, it may be interesting to enquire whence came the traditions of Cookery in this vicinity? There can be little doubt they were English, and were brought over by our Puritan mothers, in the May Flower; they were transmitted from mother to daughter almost unchanged for the hundred and fifty years of New England housewifery before the Ohio Company brought our patient, enduring grandmothers to another wilderness of new difficulties.

As to the cook's materials in the first years. The woods supplied game in abundance, but the fruits, vegetables, and grains of their old homes were lacking, and ingenuity must have been sorely taxed to produce a variety. It was at this time that one of the first settlers said of his wife: "Mrs.—— can make the best victuals out of nothing of any one I ever saw." The French chef can claim no higher praise. While in the main our cookery was English, yet some good dishes were local and peculiar.

Succotash, Pumpkin Bread and Baked Squash were no doubt inventions of the First Settlers, and long may their memory live!

A gentleman who had traveled far and wide, used to say that in Marietta were blended most happily the best of Northern and Southern ideas of cookery. There were here in early times some Southern families and some famous cooks. "Old Gin" and "Daphne" are names which recall the good things that make the mouth water.

Some excellent German dishes have been introduced. Especially have they taught us the use of salads, which are now indispensable.

Some change in culinary matters took place, under the influence of several Eastern housekeepers who were accustomed to the more finished habits of Boston and New York, and who introduced among us many new dishes of the lighter kinds and also some more modern ideas in arranging tables and serving food.

Our housewives have not departed from the teaching of their mothers. Order, system and cleanliness are still practiced, together with a high regard for the pleasures of the palate.

They have vied with each other in making the table attractive, and it is to-day no small epicurean treat to be invited to a Ladies' Luncheon, where the hostess, the china, linen, flowers and viands all combine to charm the senses.

M. N. B.

Breads, Yeast, Hot Cakes, etc.

"The very staff of life
The comfort of the husband, the pride of the wife,"

"And then to breakfast with
What appetite you have."

APPLE JOHNNIE CAKE.

MRS. LAURA CHAMBERLAIN.

One pint sour milk, 1½ pint New Orleans molasses, 1 teaspoonful soda, 2 teaspoonsful cream tartar, 1 egg well beaten, 2 tablespoonsful melted lard. Peel, core, and chop fine, 3 large Russet apples, corn meal enough to make a stiff batter. Place a paper in the bottom of a well-greased pan, bake ¾ of an hour in a moderate oven, as it burns easily.

MRS. GOVERNOR MEIGS'S BREAD. 1830.

DAPHNE C. SQUIRES.

Sift about 4 quarts of flour in a bread-bowl, add 2 teaspoons of salt, ½ pint of (Daphne's) yeast, 1 pint of luke warm milk, stir in just enough of the flour to make a thin batter. Do this the night before. Set this in the brick oven (in winter) to rise till morning. Then add to it ½ pint of warm milk, stirring in gradually the moderately warm flour, till the batter is nearly thick enough to knead. Put it in a warm place for an hour and a half, then knead it a good while, then put it in a warm place to rise again, then bake it. In the summer use water instead of milk. A little piece of butter makes bread more tender and it is well to add a little saleratus (dissolved in water) just before it is set to rise the last time.

BREAD.

MISS MARTHA PUTNAM.

Four quarts flour, 1 quart milk or water, 1 tablespoon lard or butter, 2 tablespoons sugar, 1 tea cup yeast. Put the flour into a large bowl, make a deep hollow and pour in the above, and keep in a warm place. When light mix and knead well. In an hour or two it should be light. Work into loaves and in another hour it should be ready for baking.

BREAD.

MRS. CAROLINE DANA DAWES, LINCOLN, NEB.

Three tablespoons of flour, scald with boiling water enough to make a batter, when milk warm add two or three spoonsful of yeast, a teaspoonful of sugar and a teaspoonful of salt; this will rise in 15 or 20 minutes, then use this for making your sponge,—soak your dried yeast with milk instead of water. The more you beat the sponge the better it is; when you mold up your bread the first time work it a good deal, pull and stretch as well as knead the dough. When you make it out the last time only mold enough to shape. When potato is used for making sponge use equal *quantities of potato and flour*. After making out light biscuits dip them in melted butter before baking. If you use milk in mixing up your bread, you will not need any other shortening.

BREAD.

MRS. JOHN L. BLYMYER, MANSFIELD, O.

Three pints milk, scald it well, 1 tablespoon of lard or butter, 1 tablespoon of sugar, 1 teaspoon of salt, 1 cake of Fleischman's yeast dissolved in a half cup of water, when cool add yeast and mix up stiff, cover well, let it stand all night in a warm place, then work up twice.

BOSTON BROWN BREAD.

One cup of rye meal, 2 cups of corn meal, 3 cups of sour milk (scant), ½ cup molasses, 1 tablespoon of soda, 1 teaspoon of salt. Dissolve the soda in the sour milk. Steam four hours and bake twenty minutes.

BOSTON TEA CAKE.

MRS. NAHUM WARD.

One and a half pints flour, 3 eggs, ¾ pint of sweet milk, ½ tea cup of white sugar (or less), 3 teaspoons of baking powder, ½ teaspoon of salt. Beat the eggs, melt the butter in the milk, bake quickly, say 25 minutes. Split and butter, and eat while hot.

LIGHT BREAD (USING POTATO BALL).

MRS. A. W. KING.

In the evening take 1 pint warm, mashed potatoes, add a large spoonful of white sugar, 1 teaspoonful of salt, 1 small cup of potato ball, if the potatoes are dry add a little water, (you can use potatoes left from dinner). Set this in a warm place till morning, then take 1 quart of warm water, make a thick batter by adding flour and potatoes, except a cupful which must be saved for the next baking. When the sponge rises thicken with flour. Let it rise and mould into loaves. This makes two large loaves. If 3 loaves are wanted, add another pint of water when making sponge. This is much easier and quicker made than yeastbread, and (if kept in a cool place) the potato ball need not be renewed. The potato ball is made two or three days before baking, in this way: take a pint of mashed potatoes (warm), 1 teaspoonful of salt, 1 tablespoonful of sugar, 1 cake of compressed yeast or any good yeast.

BUNS.

MISS MARY STONE. 1830.

Rub 4 ounces of butter into 2 pounds of flour, a little salt and 4 ounces of sugar, 1 dessertspoonful of caraway seed and 1 teaspoonful of ginger. Put some warm milk or cream to 4 tablespoonsful of yeast. Mix all together into a paste, but not too stiff. Cover it over and set it before the fire an hour. After this has risen make it into buns. Put them in bake pans and set them where it is warm for 15 minutes, to rise. Then brush them over with very warm milk, and bake them in a moderate oven.

DELICIOUS BROWN BREAD.

MISS MARY CUTHBERT.

One quart of sponge (white), ¾ of a cup of molasses. Work it stiff with brown flour. This will make two loaves.

BROWN BREAD.

MRS. H. D. FEARING, AMHERST, MASS.

One cup of molasses, 2 cups of water, 3 cups of sour milk, 3 cups of rye flour, 4 cups of corn meal, 1 teaspoon soda, 1 teaspoon salt. Steam 3½ hours and bake one.

BROWN BREAD.

MRS. LAURA CHAMBERLAIN.

One pint sour milk, ⅓ pint molasses, 1 pint brown flour, 1 teaspoon salt and 2 teaspoons soda.

BROWN BREAD.

MRS. WM. PITT PUTNAM.

Two quarts corn meal, 1 quart Graham flour, 1 tea cup Orleans molasses, 1 teaspoon ginger, 1 teaspoon salt, 1 pint sponge made as for light bread. Scald one-half the corn meal, mix the whole with tepid water as stiff as you can stir; let it rise, dip into pans and let rise again, bake two hours. When baked in brick oven this was allowed to remain all night and was served hot for breakfast.

BROWN LOAF.

MRS. SARAH GUITTEAU NYE.

Three cups brown flour, 3 cups corn meal, 1 cup molasses, 1 quart sour milk, 1 teaspoon soda. Boil 3 hours.

BOSTON BROWN BREAD.

MRS. H. L. HART.

Two cups corn meal, 1 cup Graham flour, 3 cups sour milk, ⅔ cup molasses, 1 dessertspoon soda, a little salt. Boil 3 hours.

BROWN BREAD (*Steamed.*)

MRS. SHAW.

One pint sour milk, ½ pint bread crumbs, ⅓ cup of molasses, 1 teaspoon of salt, 1 pint corn meal (or brown flour,) a heaping teaspoon of soda. Steam 2 hours and bake until a crust forms—perhaps half an hour.

BOSTON BROWN BREAD.

MRS. DR. SAMUEL HART.

Three cups sour milk, 2 cups corn meal, 1 cup Graham flour, ⅔ cup molasses, 1 dessertspoon soda, a little salt. Steam in a kettle over the fire. I use 1 pound baking powder cans with cover, then cover all closely. Steam 3½ hours.

BROWN MUFFINS.

MRS. ROLSTON.

One pint of milk, 3 eggs, 1 spoonful of lard, a large spoonful of molasses, 3 teaspoons of baking powder, 1 quart of flour.

MUFFINS.

MRS. DR. SAMUEL HART.

One egg, ½ cup butter and lard mixed, melted and poured into 1 pint sweet milk, 2 tablespoons baking powder, add flour enough to make a batter, not too stiff. These are excellent made of Graham flour.

CORN MEAL MUFFINS.

MRS. DR. SAMUEL HART.

Two eggs, 1 pint sour milk, 2 tablespoons sugar, ½ teaspoon soda, ½ teaspoon salt, 1 dessertspoon lard or butter, 1 cup corn meal, ½ cup flour. Bake in a quick oven.

BAKING POWDER BISCUITS.

MRS. W. W. MILLS.

One quart of flour, into which rub thoroughly 2 tablespoonsful of lard, 1 teaspoonful of salt, 3 teaspoonsful of baking powder sifted with the flour, milk enough to make a very soft dough, roll and cut. Your oven should be hot enough for your biscuits to bake in 10 minutes.

CRUSHED WHEAT.

Contributed at request of a young gentleman by

MRS. W. H. BUELL.

Get the screened wheat from the mill. Break the grains in coffee or spice mill, pick out the black specks which are the hull of another seed than the wheat. To a measure of the wheat add 3 measures of water, let it soak over night. Unless you have a kettle with water bath made for the purpose put the wheat in a tin bucket which allows for a great deal of swelling, put the tin in a kettle of cold or tepid water and bring slowly to the boiling point, where it should be kept steadily from 4 to 6 hours. The wheat will take a surprising amount of water and should not be allowed to dry off, but kept fluid by adding hot water from the tea kettle. The water bath should be kept as high as the wheat in the inner kettle. The quality prized by those who like this dish is due to the long, steady, slow cooking of the same. It should be poured into small bowls and cups to mould and is better two or three days after it is cooked.

Moses Smith sat by one day when the pot was bubbling and scalding, and sagely remarked: "It's my opinion *that* stuff is good to eat, if you have plenty of good things to eat with it," which is a fair statement of the case.

Thick cream is essential to its goodness. Most people eat it with sugar, but to some it is more digestible with cream alone.

HOME-MADE CRACKERS.

MRS. WM. PITT PUTNAM. 1830.

One quart light bread dough, butter or lard, size of an egg, 1 teaspoon of soda, dissolved. Work in all the flour possible and beat on a solid table until smooth, then take a piece, size of a walnut and work round and smooth with the thumb and finger, roll round, prick deeply, and bake at once. After baking keep in a warm oven for several hours.

CRACKER TOAST.

Heat your crackers in the stove oven. Take 1 pint of milk, 1 teaspoon salt, butter the size of a walnut, boil and pour over the crackers. Cover well and let stand 2 minutes, before serving to the table.

WAFFLES.

MRS. DR. SAMUEL HART.

Three eggs, whites and yolks beaten separately, 1 large tablespoon butter, ½ teaspoon soda, a pint of salt, 1 quart of flour with milk enough to make a batter.

DOUGHNUTS.

MRS. DR. SAMUEL HART.

Four pints flour, 2 pints sugar, 4 eggs, butter the size of an egg, 6 teaspoons baking powder. Beat the eggs in a pint cup then fill it with sweet milk.

CORN MUFFINS.

MRS. C. S. HALE.

One pint of sour milk, ½ teaspoon of soda, 1 pint of cornmeal, 1 egg, a little salt, 1 tablespoon of melted lard. Bake in sheets, or gem pans.

"EVERY DAY CORN BREAD."

MRS. GEORGE DANA.

Two or 3 eggs, 1 quart buttermilk (sour), 2 small teaspoons soda, 1 tablespoon sugar, 1 tablespoon melted butter or lard. Add sifted corn meal to make a batter which can be poured (just poured) from the jar. Bake quickly in a hot oven. Have your pans hot before putting in the bread.

CORN CAKES.

DAPHNE.

Sift meal in a pan. Pour over it some scalding hot water, not enough to thoroughly wet the meal. Four or five eggs, whites and yellows beaten separately. Milk sufficient to make thin batter. Bake on a hot griddle.

TIP-TOP CORN BREAD.

ELIZA.

Put some butter in a pan and boil it. Pour ½ this on your meal, add 1 pint sour milk, 1 teaspoon saleratus, 3 eggs. Bake in shallow pans.

DROP CAKES.

MRS. RHODES.

One pint sweet milk, 1 quart flour, a little salt, 2 teaspoonsful baking powder, melt lard, the size of a large egg and pour in when all is well beaten, drop on an iron pan, rubbed well but not greased, and bake quickly. Drop so far apart that they will not run together.

FRENCH TOAST OR FRENCH BREAD.

MRS. ISRAEL WATERS.

Four eggs, 1½ pints milk, 3 tablespoons flour, 1 teaspoon salt. Dip the bread in this mixture and fry in a pan with butter and lard.

ANOTHER: One egg, 1 teacup of milk, 1 teaspoon salt, 1 teaspoon of flour.

FRITTERS.

MRS. ISRAEL WATERS.

One pint milk, 1 quart flour, 2 eggs, 2 teaspoons baking powder. Fry in hot lard.

FRENCH ROLLS.

A HOUSEKEEPER.

Into 1 quart of sifted flour: Rub 2 rounded tablespoonsful of shortening (1 of butter and 1 of lard), then add 2 well-beaten eggs, 1 tea cup of yeast, and a little salt and sweet milk enough to make a dough. Then set to rise; let it stand till ready to make into rolls.

If wanted for tea, make up in the middle of forenoon. If wanted for breakfast, make up at 3 P. M. and make into rolls, at bed-time.

GRAHAM MUFFINS.

MRS. W. W. MILLS.

Two tea cups of Graham flour, 1 tea cup of sweet milk, 1 egg, 1 spoonful of sugar, salt, 1 spoonful of melted butter, 3 teaspoonsful baking powder. Bake in muffin rings.

GRAHAM BREAD.

MISS MARTHA PUTNAM.

One pint and a half of light sponge, scald half a tea cup of sweet milk, when cooled, stir into the sponge with a very little soda, and two or three tablespoons of sugar (more, if wished sweeter), Graham flour enough to make stiff enough to pour into the bake pan. Do not stir Graham flour more than necessary to mix well, as it makes it dry. Let it stand in a warm place till very light. If this quantity is made in one loaf it should bake about one hour.

HARESA.

MRS. E. W. LABAREE, PERSIA.

Cut into small pieces a fat chicken, from which the skin, heart, liver, etc., have been removed. Put into a large kettle with nearly a quart of hulled wheat and three or four quarts of water. Let it boil uncovered on the back of the stove six or eight hours, taking care that it does not scorch. If it becomes too stiff, add water from the tea-kettle. Do not salt it. At night, set aside in the kettle, and when it is again put on to the stove in the morning, take out the bones and beat until the meat is shredded and smoothly mixed with the wheat. Just before serving stir in a handful of salt. When dished, pour over the top a little melted butter, and thickly sift over it ground coriander seed. It should be of the consistency of mush. Cracked wheat with the fine part sifted out will answer in place of the whole grain.

HUCKLEBERRY CAKE.

MRS. ROSSITER.

Rather more than 1 cup of sugar, butter the size of an egg, 1 pint sweet milk, 1 teaspoon soda, 2 teaspoons cream of tartar, 1 quart of berries. Mix to a thick batter, and bake in a quick oven.

INDIAN BREAD.

MRS. JOHN EATON.

Scald with boiling water 1 pint of corn meal. When cool, add to this about a cup of molasses, salt, a small piece of butter or lard, or no shortening at all and yeast, then enough flour to make a pretty stiff dough, work well and set to rise. In the morning make into pans to rise again before baking. Do not have the oven too hot at first.

Breads, Yeasts, Hot Cakes, Etc.

LIGHT ROLLS.
MRS. HARRIET NYE TOWNE.

One and a half cup milk, 1 beaten egg, 1 cup yeast, 1 tablespoon white sugar, butter size of an egg. Make as stiff as can be stirred with a spoon. Roll out in the morning by merely flouring the board and pressing out with the rolling pin until you can use a cutter.

LIGHT ROLLS—VERY NICE.
MRS. MARY MCCLELLAN ADAMS.

Three or four potatoes boiled and mashed up fine in the water they are boiled in. To one pint of this potato water put in half a tea-cupful of home made yeast and let this stand until it is very light, all frothy on the top. Then make your sponge with the raised potato water. Put in two tablespoonsful of white powdered sugar, the whites of two eggs beaten stiff, and lard the size of an egg, with a little salt. When this is well raised, work it into a dough, not very stiff and let it rise. Then work it again twenty minutes and let it again rise. Then work it again twenty minutes, and cut out your rolls not making them very stiff.

LAPLAND, or BREAKFAST CAKES.
MRS. MCCANDISH.

One quart of flour, 1 quart of milk, 1 large tablespoonful of butter and lard mixed, 4 eggs, the yolks and whites beaten separately. Bake, in a quick oven. Cut in shapes.—*Norfolk.*

LAPLAND CAKES FOR BREAKFAST or TEA.
MRS. PLUNKETT.

One pint cream, 1 pint flour, 6 eggs, a little salt. Baked in shallow tins, so small as not to have to cut them.

DAPHNE'S MUFFINS.

Warm 1 quart of sweet milk with a piece of butter size of 2 eggs, beat 6 eggs (yolks and whites together), and mix with the milk, a little flour and salt, nearly ½ pint of yeast, thick with flour, as can be stirred. Made in the evening before, set to rise (for breakfast) in some warm place, in winter. If necessary, stir in a very little saleratus and water, a quarter of an hour before baking. These are stiff enough to bake as drop cakes without rings. Make a little thinner batter if you use rings.

MUFFINS.

MRS. HENRIETTE DEVOL KNOWLES.

Either white or Graham flour, 1 egg, ½ cup of sugar, 1 cup milk (sweet), butter size of an egg, 2 teaspoons of baking powder, flour to make stiff enough to chop in rings without spreading. Thoroughly mix the baking powder with the flour. Melt the butter and mix well with sugar and egg. Add the milk gradually, then stir in the flour.

LENA DE STEIGUER'S FLOUR MUFFINS.

One quart flour, 2 heaping teaspoons baking powder, 1 teaspoon salt; add water to make stiff batter as is usual for muffins. Use as cold water as possible and beat well.

MUFFINS.

MRS. T. H. HAWKS.

One tablespoon melted butter, 1 egg, 1½ cup of flour, ½ cup of sweet milk, 2 teaspoons baking powder. Bake quickly in gem pans.

MUFFINS (RAISED).

MRS. LAURA NEAL NYE.

Two eggs, 2 ounces of butter, 1 quart of flour, a teaspoonful of salt, 1 pint of sweet milk, 1 gill of yeast. Mix over night and in the morning it will be ready to drop into the muffin pans. Bake quickly.

MARYLAND BISCUIT.

MRS. SLACK.

One quart flour, 2 tablespoonsful lard, a little salt, mix with cold water taking care to make it very stiff, pound a half hour (more or less) until the dough gets very white and blisters and will snap when a piece is broken off, then break off into pieces of even size, work into biscuits, pressing in the middle with the thumb and finger, stick twice with a fork. Bake quick.

PARKER HOUSE ROLLS.

Two quarts of flour, 1 pint sweet milk, 2 tablespoons sugar, 2 tablespoons butter, ½ cup yeast, scald the milk, and after it is cool add ingredients. Make a hole in the flour and let it stand till morning. Mould it, then let it rise till noon, then make into rolls to rise for supper.

POCKETBOOKS.

MRS. SLACK.

Take a piece of bread dough about as large as a pint bowl, 2 eggs, 1 tablespoonful of lard, add enough flour to make it as stiff as it was before. *Work well.* Let it rise, and if too light work it down. An hour or so before baking, spread it out on the bread board and sprinkle over it a dessertspoonful of sugar, and a quarter of a teaspoonful of soda, dissolved in a little water, work *well* again, roll thin and grease the surface with butter, cut out and double the buttered sides together, put in baking pans and let rise again. Bake in quick oven.

PUMPKIN BREAD.

MRS. STONE.

Stew pumpkins as for pies, not quite dry, stir into the pot in which it was cooked, sugar to sweeten about as for corn bread, a teaspoonful of salt, and corn meal to make it as stiff as you can stir with a spoon. Do this at nine o'clock in the morning. Cut a paper to fit the bottom of your bread pan, then butter another one to cover the bottom and sides, put in the bread mixture and bake two hours in a slow oven, when it gets slightly brown cover it, when done keep at the back of the oven till tea time. To be eaten hot with butter. Sufficient pumpkin to fill a six quart kettle would, when stewed make about enough, with the meal, to fill a four quart bread pan.

POPOVERS.

MRS. FRAZYER.

Two eggs, 2 cups of milk, butter size of a nutmeg. Fry in hot lard and serve with sauce.

POPOVERS.

MRS. EDGERTON.

One quart of milk, butter the size of an egg, melt the butter, 2½ teaspoonsful baking powder, yolks of six eggs well beaten, 1 quart of sifted flour, whites of six eggs well beaten. Bake in hot, well greased, irons—in a quick oven.

DAPHNE'S POTATO BISCUITS.

Boil and mash four potatoes and rub together with 1 quart of flour, 1 tablespoonful of butter, add salt, milk enough to mould easily. Warm the milk and stir it with potatoes, flour, etc., add 1 tea cup of yeast. Knead 15 to 20 minutes. Let it rise till light, and then form into biscuits, with as little kneading as possible, let them rise 1½ hours or longer. Bake quickly.

RICE CAKE.
MRS. DR. COTTON. 1859.

One pint of ground rice, 1 pint of flour, 3 eggs, piece of butter size of an egg, 1 tablespoon quick yeast, 1 tablespoon sugar, a little salt, and milk enough to make a thick batter. Beat a good while and bake 30 minutes. Use Durkee's Chemical yeast.

ROLLS.
MRS. H. L. HART.

Two quarts flour, make a hole in the top, put in a piece of butter size of an egg, a little salt and a tablespoonful of white sugar; pour over this a pint of milk previously boiled and cooled and one-half teacup of good yeast. When the sponge is light, mould for 15 minutes. Let it rise again and cut into round cakes. Butter on one side and turn over on itself. Bake in a quick oven.

STEAMED BREAD.
MRS. J. H. HOBBS.

One pint of milk, 2 cups meal, 1 cup brown flour, ½ cup molasses, 1 teaspoon of soda, 1 teaspoon salt. Steam 3 hours. Bake long enough to form a crust. Can stand over night to bake in the morning for breakfast. Steam this 3½ hours if you do not wish to bake it. Let it stand two minutes with a thick cloth over it, after taking it from the steamer and it will not stick to the pan.

SPLIT CAKE.
MRS. JAMES HOLDEN.

One pint of sour milk, 1 tablespoonful of lard, melted, 1 tablespoonful of butter, melted, a pinch of salt, 1 teaspoonful of soda, flour just enough to roll out. Bake thick enough to split, and butter for the table.

NEW ENGLAND SHORT CAKE.
MRS. HOLDEN.

One pint of sifted flour, ½ teaspoonful salt (scant), ½ teaspoonful soda, one full teaspoonful cream tartar, ¼ cup of butter, measured after smoothing lump. Mix salt, soda and cream of tartar with the flour and sift twice. Rub in the butter until fine like meal, or, if liked very short and crisp, melt the butter, and add hot with the milk; add the milk gradually, mixing and cutting with a knife; divide into two parts, roll gently until about the size of a pie plate. Bake. Cut round the edge. Tear open and spread with softened butter. Fruit may be spread on if you like.

STRAWBERRY SHORT CAKE.

MRS. J. L. RECKARD.

For each cake allow 1 pint flour, 1 heaping teaspoon baking powder, shortening the size of an egg. Sift the powder thoroughly into the flour; rub in the lard, salt. Make a soft dough with sweet milk, roll and bake on a pie pan. Split and butter well. Have ready a quart of strawberries and ¾ cup sugar. Divide the berries between the middle and top, sprinkling over the sugar. Serve with sugar and cream.

DAPHNE'S SALLY LUNN.

One and a half pounds flour, 2 ounces of butter, warmed in 1 pint milk, 1 tablespoon salt, 3 well-beaten eggs, 2 tablespoons fresh yeast. Set to rise. Eat hot with butter.

SALLY LUNN.

MRS. I. H. NYE.

Seven cups flour, ½ cup butter, warm, in 1 pint sweet milk, 3 eggs, 4 tablespoons yeast, salt. Let raise four or five hours.

SALLY LUNN.

MRS. ARIUS NYE.

One cup milk, 1 pint flour, 3 teaspoonsful baking powder, 1 large spoonful of sugar, 1 egg, 1 lump of butter size of an egg, 1 salt spoon salt.

SPONGE FOR BREAD.

Sponge should be mixed in a thick stone or earthen bowl. From 2½ measures of flour to one of netting. Make your sponge at night, cover close and set in a warm place till morning. Pour a coffee cup of boiling water into the sponge in the morning, *stirring all the time*, then work in flour, and knead it three or four minutes, make into loaves, put in pans, prick it with a fork and set it to rise; when light, it cracks open upon the top, and I put it on the oven to bake.

TEA CAKES.

MRS. C. B. WELLS.

One cup sugar, 1 tablespoonful butter, 1 cup sweet milk, 2 eggs, 3 pints flour, 2 teaspoonsful baking powder.

VINEYARD CORN BREAD.

MRS. E. G. BRIGHAM.

One cup sweet milk, 1 cup corn meal, 1 cup flour, ½ cup white sugar, 1 teaspoon soda, 2 teaspoons cream of tartar, 1 teaspoon salt, 1 egg. Place flour, meal, sugar, cream of tartar in a large dish. Dissolve the soda in the milk. After mixing the flour, etc. add half the milk and the egg. Beat thoroughly and add the rest of the milk. Beat thoroughly again and bake as for layer cakes in a quick oven. (This quantity makes two layers), place one layer on the other, serve hot, cut in pie shaped pieces.

MONTANA WAFFLES.

MRS. T. A. WICKES, MONTANA.

Three-fourths cup yeast, 1 quart loppered milk, 3 tablespoonsful white sugar, 1 tablespoonful lard, 3 eggs, 1 teaspoonful salt, ½ teaspoonful soda, flour to make soft batter. Leaving out soda, mix, to rise over night. Dissolve soda in 1 tablespoonful boiling water, and add just before baking in hot greased irons, beating the batter thoroughly.

WAFFLES.

MRS. JOHNSON WELCH, ATHENS.

One and a half pints of sour milk, 1½ pints of flour, 1 teaspoonful of salt, 1 large spoonful of butter, 3 eggs, whites well beaten, 1 teaspoonful of soda. Beat together quickly, and cook a nice crispy brown over a hot fire.

WAFERS.

MRS. WHEELER, KENTUCKY.

One quart of flour, 1 tablespoonful of butter and lard mixed (or 3 ounces of butter and lard.) Mix with cold water to a stiff dough. Leave one-half of a pint of flour out of the quart of flour to work and beat into the dough. Beat and knead until it is smooth and blisters, then take a small piece of the dough and roll it as thin as you can and prick with a fork all over to keep it from blistering. Bake in a quick oven.

YEAST.

"Hear ye not the hum of mighty workings."

MRS. EDGERTON.

Six potatoes, one handful hops, tied in a thin cloth, 1 gallon water. Potatoes and hops boiled separately, same length of time. After boiling peel and mash potatoes, then strain both potatoes and hops through a colander. Afterwards add 1 teacup of salt, 1 teacup sugar, and when sufficiently cool, add 1 cup of yeast. Keep in a warm place twelve hours. Next morning it will be ready to bottle in glass fruit jars with cork stoppers.

MRS. MEIGS'S YEAST.

DAPHNE'S.

Boil 1 handful of hops in 1 quart of water for some time. Pour this (through a sieve) on to ½ pint of sifted flour, (or in winter on to mashed potatoes). Stir in more flour and beat out all the lumps. Have a sweet, clean crock and put in the yeast with 2 tablespoonsful (at least), of the old yeast. In the winter set it near the fire to rise.

YEAST.

MRS. GEO. DANA.

Three quarts water, 8 potatoes size of an egg (pared), 1 teacup hops in a bag, 1 teacup salt, 1 teacup sugar. Boil the potatoes and mash them and when cool add the yeast. Keep in a jug, corked.

YEAST.

MISS MARTHA PUTNAM.

Six good-sized potatoes boiled in 1 quart water, mash through a colander. Steep a handful of hops in 1 quart of water, and pour over potatoes, 1 teacup of sugar, 1 teacup coarse salt. When milk warm add ½ cup yeast. This will not run over when light, only bubble. Keep in glass closely covered: no soda is needed with this yeast, though the dough may have a sharp odor.

NANCY'S YEAST.

MRS. FRAZYER.

One handful of hops to about 4 quarts of water. Boil down to 3 quarts 5 tablespoonsful of sifted flour in a jar. Pour upon it the hop water strained through a colander. Boil 4 potatoes, mash and strain them and the water they were boiled in; 1 teaspoon salt, ½ cup sugar. When cool add 1 teacup of good yeast. Set in a warm place and let rise. Then put in a cool place. 1 cup of yeast for two loaves.

YEAST RECEIPT.

MRS. D. W. SHARPE.

Eight good sized potatoes, boil, peel and mash fine, 2 handsful of hops, boiled till strength all out, then strain them. 1 cup salt, 1 cup sugar, 1 gallon boiling soft water, 1 tablespoonful of ginger. When cool put in your starting yeast. Let it stand 24 hours, then put away air tight. Use ½ pint for 6 large loaves.

Roasts, Broils, Meatpies and Fish.

"*Relations always expect Meat for Breakfast.*"

HOW TO BROIL STEAK.

At the time of placing the steak over the fire, put into the oven a dripping pan large enough to hold the steak without folding. As soon as the steak is lightly browned on both sides, transfer it to the hot pan and hot oven, where, if it be thick, it will need to remain from 5 to 10 minutes.

ANOTHER WAY: Let your frying pan get smoking hot, lay your steak in smoothly without any grease or butter. It will stick fast at first but as soon as it is browned it can be loosened with a knife. When the juice begins to appear turn it over, press closely to the pan when turned, turn it every quarter of a minute until done, then pepper and salt, pressing in the butter upon a hot platter. Some add a tablespoon of coffee to make some gravy, pour in the pan and let it boil up.

"Keep the broiling pan piping hot all the time the meat is cooking."—MRS. EWING.

TO MOCK BROIL A CHICKEN IN AN OVEN.

Prepare a chicken as for broiling, by being opened down the back, wash in cold water and wipe dry with a soft cloth, flatten the breast bone with a mallet, twist the wings back to expose the breast, then place the chicken skin up in a dripping pan, press it close to the pan to make it lie as flat as possible, then put in a hot oven. In five minutes it will begin to sputter, in 20 or 25 minutes it will be cooked ready for seasoning upon a heated platter with pepper, salt and butter.
—MRS. E. P. EWING.

Have the oven just as hot as the chicken will bear without burning.

ROAST BEEF.

M. T. PEDDINGHAUS.

Put beef in a hot oven, do not salt until almost done. A moderate oven will make tender beef tough, a quick bake *without* salt will insure a tender juicy roast.

RECIPE FOR BRINE.

MRS. ROSSETER.

Five pounds salt, 5 pounds sugar, 12 quarts water, 2 ounces saltpetre, boil, skim and pour over the meat while hot.

A GOOD BRINE FOR BEEF.

MRS. W. H. GURLEY.

For 100 pounds of beef take 9 pounds of salt, 3 pounds of sugar, 2 ounces of soda, 2 ounces of saltpetre, put all into six gallons of water and boil, place the beef in a clean vessel and pour the mixture over hot.

ACCEPTABLE SUMMER DISHES—(BRAISED BEEF.)

Take a piece of rump of beef, or the chuck roast, weighing six pounds, run several strips of fat pork through the lean part with a large larding needle, bind it into shape with tape, put it into a braising pan, if you have it, if not, into a pot with a close-fitting lid.

Put two ounces of butter, half a teaspoonful of pepper and three tablespoonsful of salt into the pot, cover it, put it over a slow fire for half an hour, stirring it all round twice, then add a quart of water, leave it to very slowly cook for an hour and a half longer, then add three dozen button onions and two dozen very young carrots or large ones cut into several pieces and shaped like young ones, place these around the meat, make a bouquet of five branches of parsley, two bay leaves and two sprigs of thyme tied together; half an hour later add two dozen tiny young turnips or large white ones cut into balls. Let it now stew gently an hour and a half longer, making altogether four hours.

Take out the meat, remove tapes and trim it. Take up the vegetables and lay them in neat rows around the meat, the onions first, then the carrots, then the turnips. Put them to keep hot. Throw half a cup of ice water into the gravy to make it easy to skim, then take off all the grease. Stir in a tablespoonful of brown thickening (or of butter and flour and color with caramel if you have none ready) and a small teaspoonful of sugar. Stir gently, and when just boiling pour it round the meat through a strainer.

CODFISH BALLS.

MRS. PILLSBURY.

Soak salt fish in cold water, cut in pieces and put on the stove, let them come to a boil. Then drain off the water, draining off water several times, then pick it up, having potatoes ready. Chop together ½ fish and ½ potatoes. Beat one egg and mix in balls and fry in hot lard.

CODFISH BALLS.

MRS. C. V. CRAM.

Pick fine 1 quart of codfish, let it simmer on the back of the stove 15 minutes, then boil gently fifteen minutes; also boil 6 good-sized potatoes, mash fine to mix while hot with the fish, season with pepper and salt, add a tablespoon of butter; lastly beat three eggs well and stir through the fish and potato, drop into hot lard from a spoon or form into balls; lay a napkin on a platter to absorb the fat.

CODFISH AND EGGS.

Chop the codfish fine, simmer on the stove, changing the water once or twice, pour off water, add 1 cup of cream, just before serving, stir in 3 or 4 well beaten eggs.

CODFISH DINNER.

MRS. A. T. NYE.

Soak the fish in plenty of water, putting it in early in the morning. About an hour before dinner set it on the back of the stove and let it cook slowly but never boil it. Use boiled potatoes and boiled beets when beets are young and tender. Onions if you prefer them to beets. Drawn butter gravy and pork scraps in a separate dish as all do not relish pork. Garnish the fish with hard boiled eggs.

FISH CHOWDER.

MRS. PILLSBURY.

Fresh cod or haddock should be used, cut fish in convenient pieces, 6 slices of salt pork, fry brown in the chowder kettle, then take out the pork but leave the fat in kettle. Having some potatoes ready peeled and sliced, peel and slice 6 onions. Oyster or Boston crackers. Put layer of potatoes, layer of fish, layer of onions, some slices of pork, layer of crackers, pepper and salt, then commence over again until all is used, having crackers on the top, then put in water until you can see it. Boil until potatoes are done, then put in 1 pint of milk and boil 10 minutes.

FAMOUS RECIPE FOR CURING HAMS.

The following is the famous recipe used by Mrs. Henry Clay for curing hams, several hogsheads of which were annually sent to Boston, where, under the name of "Ashland Hams," they commanded the highest of prices, especially among the wealthy Whigs of that city;

For every 10 hams of moderate size she took 3½ pounds of fine salt, 1 pound of saltpetre and 2 pounds of brown sugar, and after mixing these thoroughly together, rubbed the hams therewith on either side. They were then packed in a tight box and placed in a cool out-house for about three weeks, when the hams were taken out and put in a pickling tub or hogshead and covered with brine strong enough to swim an egg.

After remaining in the pickle for about three weeks they were taken out, thoroughly rubbed with fresh salt and hung up in a well-ventilated house for a few days to dry. Next they were transferred to the smoke-house, where they were hung up and smoked with green hickory or walnut wood until they acquired the color of bright mahogany. This accomplished, each ham was sewed up in a canvas, the coverings whitewashed and hung up to dry, after which they were whitewashed again and packed away in hogsheads with hickory ashes, until wanted for either home use or sending to Boston.

CURING BEEF OR HAMS.

NEVER KNOWN TO FAIL.

MRS. ANSELM TUPPER NYE.

Four gallons of water, 3 pounds of salt, 1½ pounds of sugar, 2 ounces of saltpetre. Hams should remain in the brine six weeks. Rub the hams well with salt before putting them in the brine. Beef can be cured in two weeks.

CALF'S HEAD DINNER.

MRS. ANSELM TUPPER NYE.

The Calf's head and feet should be prepared by scalding and scraping, and the tongue taken out before the head is split through the middle, the brains taken out and after soaking over night put in a little bag of muslin to be boiled (15) fifteen minutes. The head, feet and harslet having been soaked for some hours in cold salted water, should be boiled in water carefully skimmed from 2½ to 3 hours until tender.

DRAWN BUTTER GRAVY FOR CALF'S HEAD.

Rub 2 ounces of butter into 1 tablespoon of flour, pour upon it either milk or water *boiling*. Stir all the time and let it boil up once only or it will be oily. Arrange all the large pieces on a platter. Chop a little of the liver with the brains and add to the gravy. Pour on the platter and garnish with parsley and hard boiled eggs. The parts around the tongue are very nice. The tongue should be skinned when done. This is a very rich dish.

FRIED CHICKEN WITH MUSH.

MRS. BETTY WASHINGTON LOVELL.

To prepare the mush take a pint of Indian meal (for four persons) and sift. Have a pint of boiling water on the fire with a teaspoonful of salt, stir in the meal a little at a time until it looks thick enough not to run. Do this early in the morning and spread to cool on a large flat dish. Cut cakes of it square or round using a little flour to handle them if necessary.

FRIED CHICKEN.

Get chickens about three months old and be sure they are fat. Cut them as for fricassee, in quarters. Dredge them with flour, and sprinkle lightly with salt. Put them to fry in a good quantity of boiling lard. They should be of a fair light brown when done. Fry small pieces of mush and lay on the bottom of the dish. Garnish the dish with cured parsley.

GRAVY.

Boil half a pint of rich milk, add to it a small bit of butter, with pepper, salt and chopped parsley. Stew it a little and serve hot with the chicken from a gravy boat.

FRIED CHICKEN.

MRS. N. D. LYON.

Cut the chicken in small pieces and remove the skin; put it in water enough to boil, to which add a little salt; when it is almost done, roll each piece in flour, sprinkle with pepper and salt, lay it in a pan, put a small lump of butter on each piece, and sufficient boiling water to baste it with. When *brown* make a gravy of the liquor the chicken was boiled in with a little flour and an egg well beaten, pour it over the chicken, put it back in the oven a few minutes, then serve.

STEWED CHICKEN WITH RICE.

MRS. J. H. CHAMBERLIN.

Cut up the chicken and stew as usual, boil a cup of rice by itself till it is done. Five minutes before the chicken is ready to take up put in the rice, with a liberal seasoning of salt, pepper (red if preferred), and butter. When done, take out the chicken first upon a platter, pour the rice and gravy through a small sieve; what goes through with the gravy will thicken it sufficiently. Place the rice remaining in the sieve, in large spoonsfull around the edge of the platter. Save the gravy by itself in gravy boat.

CHICKEN PIE.

MRS. GEO. M. WOODBRIDGE.

Prepare one chicken. One-half pound or less of fresh pork or spare rib. If the chicken is young stew it half an hour, well covered with water. Season it to your taste with pepper and salt. Thicken the gravy with two teaspoons of flour, wet with milk or water. Have a deep pan lined with rather plain pie crust, rolled moderately thin. The upper crust should be a rich one, fully half an inch thick with openings cut entirely through to the chicken to allow gases to escape. Place the poorer parts of the chicken at the bottom of the pan, the better on top. Pour over the chicken all the gravy with bits of butter laid on the fowl. Add the upper crust, press firmly to prevent gravy from escaping and bake an hour in a moderate oven. If a cup is placed upside down in the dish before putting in the chicken, the gravy will be drawn into it, and not run out while baking. Remove cup before serving.

FOR CORNING BEEF AS IT BOILS — Very Nice for Tongues.

MRS. C. B. WELLS.

For six pounds beef take: 1 gallon water, 1 pint salt, 1 teacup sugar, 1 teaspoonful soda, ¾ teaspoonful saltpetre. Boil three or four hours, or till done. Keep filling the kettle with boiling water as it boils away.

DRESSING FOR TURKEY.

MRS. H. L. HART.

Two pounds bread, crumbed fine, 6 ounces butter, 2 tablespoons sage, pulverized, 1 small onion, sliced fine, salt and pepper to taste, 2 teacups cream.

See "Oysters" for oyster dressing.

DRAWN BUTTER.

Rub 2 teaspoonful of flour into a quarter of a pound of butter, add 5 tablespoonsful of cold water, set it into boiling water and let it melt, and heat until it begins to simmer, when it is done. Never simmer it on coals, as it fries the oil and spoils it. If to be used with fish add chopped eggs and nasturtions or capers. If used with boiled fowls, put in oysters and let them heat through.

DRIPPINGS.

French cooks prefer beef fat to lard for frying. Beef fat does not adhere to articles cooked in it and does not impart flavor, and frying done in beef fat is more wholesome and digestive than when done in lard. A careful cook need never buy fat for the frying kettle, but will find herself amply supplied with the drippings from roasts of beef and the fat skimmed from the soup kettle. These skimmings and remnants should be tried out twice a week by boiling them all together in water. When the fat is all melted it should be strained with the water and set away to cool. When it has hardened lift the cake from the water, scrape off every dark particles adhering at the bottom, melt again and strain into a small stone jar, it is now ready for use. Miss Corson says after drippings are tried out or cleansed they will keep as well as butter or lard. They are cheaper than good butter and in general estimation preferable to lard. "Each kind should be kept in separate vessels and used with reference to the flavor they impart, as they have marked individual flavors."

A VERY NICE WAY TO COOK A FLANK OF BEEF.

MRS. M. L. GODDARD.

After washing and wiping, season the surface with pepper, salt and a little sage, roll tight and sew up in a cloth. Put a broken plate in the bottom of the kettle and lay the meat on it. Then boil several hours till well done. Take out and press before removing the cloth. When perfectly cold, the cloth can be taken off and the meat will be solid and cut into nice slices.

TO COOK MACKEREL.

MRS. M. L. GODDARD.

Soak, skin side up 24 hours changing the water at least once. Wipe dry and hang up over night. In the morning fry, putting the skin side *down* first, then turn and fry brown.

MEAT—FRESH.

"The economical way of cooking meat is to boil it gently in a close pot, where the steam will condense on the inside of the cover and fall back upon the meat." "The shoulder piece of beef can be made into a tender and delicate dish by letting it cook in its own juices in the oven without one particle of water. A stone jar with a tight-fitting cover (or a lid of plain dough) will keep in all the flavor and the juices. It will require 3 or 4 hours. The heat that comes through the stone is very different from that of iron. It is the slow action of the steady heat that makes a rich dish out of a cheap joint."

TO PICKLE TONGUE OR BEEF.

MRS. S. P. HILDRETH.

Four gallons of water, 1½ pounds of sugar, 3 ounces of saltpetre, 8 pounds of salt. Boil, skim when cold, and pour over your meat.

(This is Mrs. Rhoda Cook's recipe, and is probably nearly 100 years old.)

TO PICKLE BEEF AND TONGUE.—(VERY GOOD.)

MRS. EMMA CADWALLADER.

Two gallons water, 3 pounds salt, 1 ounce of saltpetre, 1 pound of sugar or 1 pint of molasses. Boil all together, skim and pour over the meat when cold.

PERSIAN STEW.

MRS. E. W. LABAREE, PERSIA.

Two pounds of meat, fat and lean together, cut into small bits, 2 medium sized onions chopped, put all into a kettle with ½ cup of cold water, set over a hot fire and stir frequently until the meat and onions are well browned. If in danger of burning add a spoonful of water from time to time. When well browned add ¼ can of tomatoes, salt, pepper, (cayenne is best) and 2 quarts or more of hot water. Set the kettle back where it will stew slowly but constantly for at least two hours. Half an hour before serving pour in ½ cup of uncooked rice. Should it dry away too much add a little water. Any kind of meat can be used, but the best stew is made from mutton or veal.

PICKLE FOR BEEF OR TONGUE.—(OLD.)

MRS. MARTHA BRAINARD WILSON.

Six pounds of salt, 1½ ounzes of saltpetre, 1½ pounds of brown sugar, for 100 pounds of meat. Water sufficient to cover. Put the meat in weak salt and water over night, drain thoroughly in the morning and pack in a tub, or a sugar barrel is better, and cover with the prepared brine. Water fresh from the well with the sugar, salt, and saltpetre thoroughly stirred in and dissolved, then add as much water as necessary to cover.

STEWED CHICKEN.

MRS. A. G. GARD, VINCENT.

Take a good sized chicken, cut it up, put it to cook, after skimming add pepper and salt to taste, when *nearly* done add one cup of butter, when *done* take milk or cream with enough flour to make plenty of gravy, have some nice baking powder biscuit hot, break in two or three pieces and pour the gravy over—we think it nice.

SAUSAGE.

MRS. WM. PITT PUTNAM, BELPRE.

To 50 pounds of prepared sausage add 1 pound and 2 ounces of salt, 5 ounces of pepper, 4 ounces of sage. Season before grinding pork.

SAUSAGE.

MISS MARY SLACK, KY.

Twenty pounds of pork before it is prepared, 1 small teacup of salt, 5 tablespoonsful of pulverized sugar, 5 tablespoonsful of black pepper, 1 teaspoon cayenne pepper. Season after it is ground.

SAUSAGE — OLD.

MRS. BENJAMIN DANA.

Twenty pounds of meat, ½ pound salt, 2 ounces of sage, 2 ounces of pepper. Sprinkle over the meat before grinding.

ROAST TURKEY — NEW STYLE.

SOUTH CH. COOK BOOK.

After drawing the turkey rinse with several waters and in next to the last mix a teaspoon of soda. Fill the body well with soda water, shake well, empty, rinse in fair water. Then prepare a dressing of bread crumbs mixed with butter, pepper, salt and such sweet herbs as you like wet with either milk or water. Add, if you choose, the beaten yolks of two eggs. Some like oysters chopped and put in the dresssing. Stuff the craw and body and sew up with a strong thread; dredge with flour and rub with salt, and place a buttered paper over it to prevent its browning too soon. Baste often and roast from four to five hours according to size. The giblets may be cooked separately and chopped to be added to the gravy.

ROAST TURKEY — Old Style.

MRS. FAY.

A large turkey dressed and stuffed with bread crumbs, seasoned with salt pork, sage, and whole cloves. This was then hung before an open wood fire with a pan under to catch the drip. Cook from three to five hours according to the size of the turkey, basting and turning every little while. "Never was anything half so nice as turkeys, chickens and geese roasted in this way."

SOUPS.

"Every cook praises his own stew."

BEZIQUE SOUP.

MISS GRACE CRAM.

One quart can of tomatoes, 3 pints of boiling water, 1 teaspoon of soda, boil half an hour, 4 tablespoons of butter, 2 tablespoons of flour, 1 tablespoon salt, cream together. ½ teaspoon celery seed. Heat 1 quart new milk add and strain. This soup can be made quickly.

BEEF SOUP.

MRS. H. B. SHIPMAN.

Put on early in the morning in about 6 quarts of cold water, a good sized shin piece. Boil slowly all the forenoon. If necessary replenish with boiling water. At noon add 2 quarts of tomatoes, 4 potatoes, 3 onions, 2 small turnips, all sliced thin, a little cabbage and any other vegetable you may like. Boil 4 hours longer, stirring frequently the last hour or two. One hour before removing from the fire put in a teacupful of rice. Strain through a colander and set away to cool. The next morning it will be jellied and you can easily remove the cake of fat from the surface. In cold weather this will keep for days. To prepare for the table, add a little water, season with salt and pepper, boil up once, and serve hot.

BOUILLON OF BEEF.

Six pounds of brisket or round of beef all in one piece, 4 turnips, 3 carrots, 2 Bermuda onions, a good handful of cabbage sprouts, 2 tablespoonsful of butter, cut up in flour, bunch of sweet herbs, 1 teaspoonful of made mustard, 4 quarts of water. Cover the beef with the water, and cook slowly 1 hour. Meanwhile cut the vegetables into long strips, not too thin, leaving the sprouts whole. Cook them all in boiling salted water 20 minutes. Throw this water away, and at the end of the hour skim the soup well, and put in the vegetables. Stew all very slowly 2 hours longer. There must never be a fast boil. Take out the beef, put into a dripping pan, pour a cup of the soup (strained) seasoned well with pepper, salt, and mustard over it, dredge thickly with flour, and brown in a good oven, basting every few minutes. Take one-half of the vegetables from the pot, and keep hot. Rub the rest through a colander, season the soup and pulp, add the herbs and return to the sauce pan, boil sharply for 5 minutes, stir in butter and flour, simmer 5 minutes, and your soup is ready for the tureen. Season the reserved vegetables, and having dished your beef, lay them very hot around it. Serve with each slice.

BOUILLON.

One and one-half pounds of beef, 3 quarts of water, 1 ounce of salt, 3 leaks, 2 cloves, ½ head of celery, ¼ of a parsnip. Serve, after straining clear.

BOUILLON.

FOURTH ST. COOKING CLUB.

Bone of a round of beef, 4 quarts of water (cold). Boil down to 3 quarts by simmering gently *all day*, skimming as in other soup. Season with salt. Let it stand and cool until the fat can be taken off. When heated for use, season to taste with cayenne pepper. This makes an amber colored soup. If darker is desired use more mea

BLACK BEAN SOUP.

MRS. DAVID KING, AKRON.

Put one quart of beans to soak over night, boil five hours with 3 pounds of beef, 1½ pounds pork, 1 head of celery, 2 grated carrots, cloves, allspice, cinnamon, salt, pepper, put in tureen. 2 hard boiled eggs sliced, 1 lemon sliced, 1 tablespoon tomato catsup, 2 slices of toast cut in squares. Strain the soup on this.

CHERRY SOUP.

MRS. JOHN CONLEY, CHICAGO.

One and a half quarts of cherries, 3 pints of water, boil 1 quart of cherries until the cherries are pulpy, sweeten to taste and strain. Stone the ½ quart cherries and with a half teacup of sago put into the soup and boil until the sago is clear, not dissolved. Serve cold.

CONSOMME SOUP.

MRS. H. WHITNEY.

Four pounds of shank of beef with sinew, 1 knuckle of veal without meat, have bones mashed at meat market, 1 small carrot, 1 turnip, 1 onion, 1 bunch celery, 1 bunch parsley, 12 cloves, 40 black pepper corns.

Put meat on back of stove till it begins to boil, then boil half an hour on front of stove. Next put in vegetables and boil hard one hour, then put on back of stove and simmer steadily six hours. Add 2 gallons of water, and if not enough add 2 quarts more — or if not rich enough after it is strained simmer down. Can be used several days.

CLEAR SOUP.

MRS. WASHINGTON GLADDEN.

Five pounds of beef cut from under part of round, 5 quarts of cold water, cut beef into small pieces, add water, let it come to a boil very gradually, skim and set back where it will keep to boiling point, (very slight motion,) 8 hours. Then strain through a colander, and set away to cool. In the morning skim off all fat, and turn soup into a soup kettle, being careful to keep back sediment, add 1 onion, 1 stalk of celery, 2 sprigs of parsely, 2 of thyme and savory, 2 leaves of sage, 2 bay leaves, 12 pepper corns, 5 whole cloves. Boil gently from 10 to 20 minutes, then strain through an old napkin, and it is ready for use.

CORN SOUP.

Boil a small shank of beef in 2 quarts of water for 2 hours. After it has boiled an hour and a half, add salt, 4 good sized tomatoes, and 8 ears of corn, cut, and scrape from the cob. Fifteen minutes before serving add 1 quart of milk and a lump of butter the size of an egg, and some pepper, and 4 powdered crackers. Canned corn and tomatoes can be used in the winter.

GREEN PEA SOUP.

MRS. OSCAR MITCHELL.

One quart milk, 2 large cupsful peas, 1 tablespoonful butter, 1 heaping tablespoonful flour. Salt and pepper. Into the boiling milk pour mashed peas, butter and flour *creamed*. Season and strain.

GUMBO SOUP.

MRS. M. P. WELLS.

Put into a skillet one good sized onion and a slice of ham cut very fine. Fry them brown with a small piece of butter. When brown put in a chicken and a veal cutlet cut into small pieces, and a half pound of dried gumbo or one pound of green gumbo. Add a saltspoonful of cayenne pepper and salt to taste. Let it fry for half an hour, then turn it into a pot containing about 4 quarts of boiling water. Boil for an hour or more replenishing with boiling water if necessary. Serve with boiled rice.

JULIENNE SOUP. — With Variations.

MRS. EDGERTON.

Procure 5 or 6 pounds of lean beef, season with salt only. Put it in a soup kettle with 5 quarts of cold water, bring it to a boil, then set aside to simmer, closely covered, for 6 or 8 hours, or until the meat falls from the bones. Strain it and set aside until next day, when carefully remove all the fat from the top. Add a pint of cold water, 1 carrot cut in small pieces, 1 turnip the same, 1 potato sliced thin, 2 onions in rings, 5 tomatoes peeled and cut up, and half a cup of barley or rice. Bring all to a hard boil, then simmer slowly, closely covered for three hours. Season to the taste with pepper and salt. The barley or rice can be left out, and 1 root of celery cut up into very small pieces substituted.

MOCK TURTLE SOUP — With Variations.

MRS. EDGERTON.

Procure a fine large calf's head, cleanse the head thoroughly, tie the brains up in a cloth, put all together into a soup kettle, with five quarts of cold water, and one tablespoonful salt. Bring to a boil and skim well, then set aside to simmer slowly for three hours. The brains will be done in one hour and must be taken out and set aside. When you can twist out the bones remove the kettle from the fire and strain through a colander. Put the broth back in the soup pot, take out all the bones from the meat, cut it into small pieces, reserve a cup full of it and set it aside, season the remainder with half a teaspoonful of black pepper, a teaspoonful of sweet marjoram, the same quantity of summer savory, an onion chopped, a teaspoonful of powdered cloves and two blades of mace. Stir all well together and put it into the broth, add a bunch of parsley and thyme, cover closely and simmer for an hour and a half, then strain and set away for the next day. Next morning prepare forced meat balls as follows: Chop very fine one pound of lean uncooked veal, and a quarter of a pound of fresh beef suet, stir them together, add a small teacup of the brains and the same of fine bread crumbs, season with half a teaspoonful of salt, a saltspoonful of black pepper, half a saltspoonful of grated nutmeg, a piece of onion the size of half a nutmeg, chopped very fine, and a teaspoonful of chopped parsley, mix all well together. Break up two eggs, stir them in. Flour your hands and make into little balls half the size of a walnut, brown them in butter and lard, drain them on a sieve or cloth and keep them hot until the soup is ready. Take all the fat from the top of the soup, put it over the fire and let it come to a boil, put in the cup of meat you reserved, thicken with a tablespoonful browned flour, mixed in cold water, boil five minutes longer. Put the forced meat balls into the tureen with several slices of lemon, pour the soup over and serve. "*Fit for a king.*"

MOCK TURTLE SOUP.

MISS ELIZABETH WOODBRIDGE, CHILLICOTHE.

Cut a calf's head, dressed from the butchers, in four parts, the skull from the lower jaw and again in two, soak in cold water 2 or 3 hours, put the brains in and tie it together, add salt and boil in a pot of water until the meat falls off, skim as soon as it boils, and then throw in two potatoes and two onions chopped, a handful of chopped parsley and a bunch of thyme twigs, two tablespoons of mixed spices, (allspice, cloves, nutmeg, mace, cinnamon and black pepper.) Take out the bones and some of the meat, a quarter of a pound of butter with two tablespoons of flour mixed together added. Boil hard two eggs, chop fine the whites, and just before serving mash the yolks very fine and make into little eggs with flour. The breast of veal with meat-heads made in the same way is a good substitute.

MOCK OYSTER SOUP.

MRS. OSCAR MITCHELL.

Grate the corn fine. To a dozen ears add 1 quart of water; boil 15 minutes, add ⅔ of a quart of milk and 1 tablespoonful of corn starch or flour, and boil 10 minutes, add ¼ pound butter and season well with pepper and salt.

MOCK BISQUE SOUP.

GRACE MAY THOMAS.

One can of tomatoes (strained), 1 quart of sweet milk, 1 teaspoonful of soda, season with pepper and salt, add 2 teaspoonsful of corn starch just as it begins to boil. Pour into the tureen and add butter the size of an egg. Twice the above quantity of butter makes it better.

OYSTER SOUP.

MRS. MCCANDISH, PARKERSBURG.

Put one quart of water in a vessel with a slice of bacon, let it boil, then add one quart of oysters with one tablespoonful of fine black pepper, four ounces of butter, three tablespoonsful of flour, one tablespoonful sweet cream, and salt enough to season it. After boiling it ten minutes longer add the yolks of two eggs well beaten and let the boiling continue about fifteen minutes longer. Take the bacon out and the soup is ready to be served.

OYSTER SOUP.

MRS. S. MILLS ELLSTON, CRAWFORDSVILLE.

One can of oysters, 1 quart of milk, 1 dozen crackers rolled, boil oyster liquor and 1 pint of cold water together, when it comes to a boil stir in the milk and oysters, butter and crackers, add salt and pepper. Serve hot.

OYSTER SOUP.

MRS. WASHINGTON GLADDEN, COLUMBUS.

One quart of oysters, if solid, wash in 1 quart of cold water, if liquid, in 1 pint. Drain water through a colander into a kettle, let come to a boil, skim carefully. Put 1 quart of milk on to boil, when it boils, thicken with two tablespoonsful of corn starch mixed with a little cold milk, then add boiling liquor of oysters, ½ cup of butter and the oysters. Season to taste and serve.

POTATO SOUP.

MRS. ROSSETER.

Boil in 2 quarts of water (more or less) 6 or 8 large potatoes. Mash the potatoes when done, or crush with a spoon, salt and pepper well. Then add 2 quarts milk and a large lump of butter, let boil. Less milk and some cream is better. When boiling stir in a few cracker crumbs, and when ready for table drop in some Boston crackers split in two.

TOMATO SOUP.

MISS ANDERSON.

One quart sifted tomato, 1 quart new milk, 1 teaspoon soda, a large piece of butter, salt, pepper. Heat the tomato and milk separately. When each has boiled put the soda in the tomato, stir and mix with the milk. Pour over broken cracker.

TAPIOCA SOUP.

MRS. EDGERTON.

Boil a soup bone very slowly 6 hours, add 1 pint tomatoes boiling all together 20 minutes. Then strain and add half a teacupful of tapioca, after it has been soaked half an hour, in clear water. Let the whole boil half an hour and serve. A little celery (chopped fine) is a great addition.

VEGETABLES.

"If you confine a man to one article of food he will not take enough to keep up natural forces."

HINTS FOR COOKING VEGETABLES.

Summer vegetables are best cooked on the same day as gathered.

Wash and prepare for cooking, and let them lie in cold water some time before using them, excepting corn and peas.

To retain green color keep uncovered whilst cooking.

Always put vegetables into boiling water and keep boiling gently until done.

The time required varies, according to the age and size, but let them cook until tender.

Asparagus requires from 30 to 60 minutes. The white part of Asparagus never boils tender. Throw it away and use only the green.

Beans-String.—Anywhere from 3 to 4 hours. Some use soda, $\frac{1}{2}$ a teaspoon is sufficient.

Beans-Shell.—1 hour to $1\frac{1}{2}$ hour. Boil in as little warm water as will keep from burning.

Beets.—Young beets will boil in $\frac{1}{2}$ an hour, but as they grow older will need from 1 to 3 hours. Leave at least 2 inches of the tops, and do not break off the little fibres or the juices will be lost.

Carrots.—In summer $\frac{3}{4}$ hour. In winter $1\frac{1}{2}$ hour.

Corn.—Boil in as little water as possible from 20 minutes to half an hour. When you cut off the corn put on the cobs in cold water, and when they have boiled take them out and put in the corn and boil until tender.

Cabbage.—In summer from $\frac{1}{2}$ an hour to 1 hour. In the winter about 2 hours. It is best to soak in salt water, and change the water in which it is boiled once or twice.

Cauliflower.—Plunge the heads in salt water to remove the insects, boil from 30 minutes to 1 hour.

Greens.—Dandelions boil 1 hour. Spinach boil 20 minutes. Always put salt in the water. The young tops of mustard, cabbage, beets, turnip, narrow dock and sorrel all make good greens and need to boil from 30 to 60 minutes.

Onions.—From 30 to 60 minutes. Change water once. Ochra boil 20 minutes.

Potatoes.—Bake potatoes of a medium size about half an hour in a steady oven, small potatoes less time, and large ones more. Serve in a hot *uncovered* dish. Baked potatoes should be the last thing to be lifted and eaten immediately. If they have to stand stick them with a fork to let out the steam. To boil let them remain in from $\frac{1}{2}$ to $\frac{3}{4}$ of an hour, according to size.

Stewed Tomatos should be cooked from $\frac{1}{2}$ to 1 hour. The longer the better. Baked tomatos with bread crumbs 1 hour.

Salsify.—From 40 to 50 minutes, boil until tender.

Winter Squash.—Steam an hour and a half.. Summer Squash will cook in one half an hour..

ASPARAGUS.

Cut the green part of asparagus in inch lengths. Boil from $\frac{1}{2}$ to $\frac{3}{4}$ of an hour. Use only water enough to cook it. Dress with a tablespoonful of butter worked into a teaspoonful of flour, 1 teaspoonful of salt. It is very nice served on toast.

BOSTON BAKED BEANS.

Put 1 quart of small white beans in bean jar. Parboil, and drain off the water. Then add $\frac{1}{2}$ pound of ham, smoked fat and lean, salt, pepper, 1 teaspoonful of ground mustard, and 3 large spoonsful of Orleans molasses. Cover all with plenty of water and put them in the oven and bake slowly for 24 or 36 hours. If they are placed in the oven Friday night they are in nice condition for Sunday morning breakfast.

BOSTON BAKED BEANS.

MRS. PILLSBURY.

Take 1 quart beans, soak over night. In the morning drain off the water and replace with fresh. Let boil $\frac{1}{2}$ an hour, drain again, then place in an earthern jar smaller at the top than bottom. Add a piece of raw salt pork and 2 tablespoonsful of Orleans molasses, salt a little, then cover with water and let boil away four times, having the beans covered all the time until you put the last water in, then remove the cover and let brown, when done they should be of a light brown color.

BAKED CORN.

MRS. ISRAEL DEVOL.

Slice off the tops of kernels and scrape the remainder of the corn out. For 1 quart of corn take 1 large teaspoonful of salt, half cup of butter, 1 coffee cup of rich milk or cream, bake 1 hour in slow oven.

ESCALOPED CABBAGE.

MRS. ISRAEL DEVOL.

Chop the cabbage as for slaw, then put a layer of it in a bake pan, then a layer of stale bread crumbs, sprinkle on salt, pepper, and lumps of butter, then another layer of cabbage an inch thick, another layer of crackers or bread, salt, pepper and butter, till the pan is full, having the crumbs etc. on top. Put in a tea cup of milk and bake one hour.

TO COOK CABBAGE WITHOUT ODOR.

FROM "TEN DOLLARS ENOUGH."

Cut the cabbage in quarters, wash and lay in colander to drain, have your kettle ready with *boiling* water, enough to cover the cabbage well, put in the cabbage and add 1 tablespoon of salt and a scant half teaspoon of soda. As soon as it comes to the boiling point take off the cover, and leave it off all the while, pushing the cabbage under the water from time to time. Boil 25 minutes. The whole secret of boiling cabbage without filling the house with a bad odor, is—*rapid boiling, plenty of water, plenty of room, and the cover off.*

CORN OYSTERS.

MRS. I. H. NYE.

To a pint of grated corn, young and sweet, add 1 egg well beaten, a small teacup of flour, ½ gill cream, 1 teaspoonful of salt, mix well and fry like oysters, dropping into fat by spoonsful.

MOCK OYSTERS.

MRS. FRAZYER.

One and one half dozen ears sweet corn, grate as fine as possible. Mix with the grated corn 3 large tablespoonsful sifted flour, yolks of 6 eggs well beaten, beat well. Have in frying pan an equal proportion of lard and butter. When boiling hot drop in portions of the mixture, as nearly as possible the size and shape of oysters. Fry them brown and serve hot. They should be nearly an inch thick.

CORN OYSTERS.

MRS. I. R. WATERS.

Grate the corn from 1 dozen ears, mix with the yolks of 6 eggs and 3 tablespoons of flour. Season with salt and pepper. Fry in hot lard, the cakes the size of oysters.

CORN FRITTERS.

MRS. W. W. MILLS.

One teacupful of sweet corn cut from the cob, 2 tablespoons of sweet milk, 1 pinch of salt, 1 tablespoonful of melted butter, flour (into which has been sifted $\frac{1}{2}$ teaspoonful of baking powder) enough to make a batter. Drop from a spoon into hot lard. Good for breakfast, dinner, or tea.

CUCUMBERS.

Pare and cut very thin; salt them well, pour on enough water to cover them; let them stand five or ten minutes, or until you wish to use them; before serving, pour off all the water, add vinegar and pepper.

EGG PLANT.

Cut in slices, about half an inch thick, sprinkle with salt, and let stand half an hour; wash in cold water, and wipe dry. Dip in a well beaten egg, then in bread or cracker crumbs, and fry in hot butter.

. TO COOK MACCARONI.

Boil in water with a little salt, a half hour or till tender. Drain. Butter a pudding dish and put in a layer of maccaroni, add pepper and salt, lumps of butter and grated cheese; continue until the dish is full. Bake $\frac{3}{4}$ of an hour.

ESCALOPED ONIONS.

Slice onions as for frying; cook them in water a few minutes; turn off water and put in a layer of onions in a pan, add a layer of bread crumbs, season as you put them in with salt and pepper, butter, cream or milk. Put them in the oven and let brown. Very nice.

PARSNIPS.

Scrape, and boil in salt and water, till tender. Cut in thick slices lengthwise, and fry brown.

PEAS.

Always wash them before shelling. Boil the fresh pods fifteen minutes in water enough to cover them. Skim out and put in the peas, and boil about a half hour.

FRENCH PEAS.

MRS. W. S. NEWTON, GALLIPOLIS.

One tablespoon of butter, put into the kettle, and two small onions cooked in this about ten minutes, and then put in water enough to boil the peas. When done, season with salt, pepper and a little sugar.

CREOLE PEAS.

Throw pea-pods into boiling water, cook to a pulp; mash through a colander and serve hot, with butter, pepper and salt. It makes a delicious, marrowy dish.

IRISH WAY OF COOKING POTATOES.

"If I should cover them with water, they'd be drowned, poor things, and would'nt be at all maly; and if I was to put biling water on 'em, they'd be waxy. I stews 'em.—It takes a time to understand a petaty: They don't like much water."

STUFFED POTATOES.

Select fine, large potatoes, and bake until tender. Cut off the ends, scoop out the contents with the handle of a spoon and work soft with butter, hot milk, pepper, salt and, if desired, a little grated cheese. Return the mixture to the skins, mounding it up on the open ends, and with these uppermost, set the potatoes in the oven five minutes. Eat from the skin.

ESCALOPED SWEET POTATOES.

MRS. P. W. SCOTT.

Parboil the potatoes and slice them lengthwise. Lay in a baking dish with a little sugar, nutmeg, and small pieces of butter between each layer. Pour a cup of milk over all, and bake a light brown. The sugar and nutmeg must be on the top layer, as with the milk, they form a brown crust.

SARATOGA POTATOES.

MISS ALICE WATERS.

Select large potatoes—small ones will do but large slices can be handled in less time than small ones. It is not *necessary* to pare the potatoes, though of course they are nicer with the skin removed. Slice very thin, from 70 to 90 slices to a large potato, with a bread-slicer or slaw-cutter, if you have one, and drop into salt water (about a teaspoonful of salt to a quart of water). Let them lie in the water for half an hour, longer will not hurt them. Then dry a handful at a time in a towel—just rubbing them lightly so as to take off most of the water. Have a skillet full of hot lard—so hot that the potato will sputter a little when dropped in. *Then drop the slices in separately* and if they fold over, unfold them with a fork, as they will hold the lard if folded or laid together. Put in enough to well cover the top of the lard, and when the edges of the slices are crisp, turn them with a fork and the middle will fry faster. When crisp, remove with a wire strainer and let drain for a few minutes, then spread on heavy brown paper, which will absorb drops of lard which might not have drained off. The lard must be *quite hot* for frying or the chips will not drain well. Before removing from the paper to a dish, sprinkle a little fine salt over them. It takes no longer to drop the slices into the lard separately and keep them flat than to put in a handful and stir with a fork. They fry faster if kept separate and unfolded.

One pound of potatoes, before being sliced, will make *about* half a pound when fried.

For an ordinary tea one pound of chips will serve about twenty-five persons. New potatoes fry much nicer than old ones.

The starch which settles in the water that the slices lie in is beautiful for laundry purposes if washed and strained.

STEWED POTATOES.

Slice rather thick, cold boiled potatoes, pour in enough milk to make them very moist, cover and let it boil until the milk is nearly

Vegetables.

boiled out. Season with butter, salt and pepper, and with a knife chop fine. Serve hot.

SOUTHERN POTATOES.

Pare and slice thin the number of potatoes wanted, let them stand in cold water ½ hour, then put them into a pudding dish, season with salt and pepper, pour on a cup of milk. Bake an hour. On taking them out, add a piece of butter the size of an egg.

PLAIN PILAV.

MRS. E. W. LABAREE, PERSIA.

Soak a pint of rice for an hour. Drain and pour into a kettle containing 2 or 3 quarts of *boiling* water and cook until the rice is tender. Do not stir or even put a spoon into it. When done turn into a colander, pour a dipper of cold water over it to wash off the starch and let it stand until the water has run off, shaking it gently, then return it to the hot kettle, in the bottom of which there should be a large spoonful of melted butter. Pour over the top of the rice through a strainer, at least ½ cup of melted butter. Cover the kettle closely with a heated lid, (a tin plate holding hot ashes is good.) Set it on the back of the stove, or on the hearth where it will keep hot, and let it stand fifteen minutes. It should be served on a platter, and when successfully made, each kernel of rice is unbroken, though thoroughly cooked, and no grains adhere together.

TO BOIL RICE.

MARTHA J. DANLEY.

Take ¾ cup of rice, wash the flour out and put water in sufficient to start it well to boiling, after which keep filling in with milk until it has cooked slowly nearly an hour. Just before taking up add ¾ cup of sugar, butter the size of a hulled walnut, and lastly, beat up an egg and stir it in. It will be ready to take up as soon as it comes to a boil.

RIPE TOMATO DOLMA.

MRS. E. W. LABAREE, PERSIA.

Cut fair, firm ripe tomatoes in two, without peeling, remove the seed and pulp. Fill with forced meal, made of uncooked rice and finely chopped bits of cold roast, seasoned with pepper, salt and chopped celery and dill or caraway leaves. Replace the tops of the tomatos and fasten with splinters. Stew for half or three-quarters of an hour in water enough to cover them, and add a bit of butter before taking up.

GREEN TOMATO DOLMA.

MRS. E. W. LABAREE PERSIA.

Cut a piece of somewhat fat raw meat into very small bits, add a little chopped onion and stir the mixture in a skillet until slightly browned. Set aside to cool. Add twice the quantity of uncooked rice, season with pepper, salt and a few leaves of celery and dill or caraway; cut very fine, mix thoroughly. Cut fair, green tomatoes in two and remove the seed and pulp without breaking the form of the fruit Fill with the forced meat and replace the top, fastening it on with splinters. Lay the tomatoes into a kettle, cover with water and stew gently until tender. While cooking add a little acid, either a cluster of green grapes, lemon juice or citric acid.

Green Cucumber Dolma is made in the same way, except that it requires more acid than the tomato.

STEWED TOMATOS.

Pour boiling water on the tomatos and remove the skin, cut in slices, and stew a half hour or longer, add butter, pepper, salt and sugar to taste, crumb up bread and thicken with it.

GREEN STEWED TOMATOS.

Pare off the skin, slice and cook with one sliced onion. Season same as ripe stewed tomatos.

ESCALOPED TOMATOS.

Prepare tomatos same as for stewing. Put a layer of tomatos in baking dish and cover with a layer of bread crumbs, some bits of butter, salt and pepper, continue this until the dish is full, finishing with bread crumbs. Bake 1 hour. Some think it is improved by adding a few small slices of onion.

TURNIPS.

Peal, cut in slices and boil till tender in salt and water *about* a half hour. When done drain through a colander, mash fine, add butter, pepper and salt if not already salt enough, *add a little white sugar.*

BAKED TOMATOS.

A BREAKFAST DISH.

MRS. DR. SAMUEL HART.

Cover the bottom of a shallow earthern dish that can be placed on the table with ripe tomatos, cut in halfs, turning the skin side downward, as it forms a cup to hold butter, pepper, and salt, cover with fine rolled bread crumbs. Bake one-half hour.

RICE CROQUETTES.

Boil 1 cup of rice without stirring in 1 quart of milk or water till quite dry, add a piece of butter the size of an egg, 2 eggs. Make into rolls (or any shape desired), dip into cracker crumbs, fry in lard.

BEVERAGES.

"And lucent Syrups tinct with Cinnamon."

"THE CUP WHICH CHEERS."

FRENCH COFFEE.
MRS. F. F. OLDHAM.

One pint of ground coffee, to 2 quarts of boiling water. Put the coffee into the uppermost compartment of a French coffee pot and pour the water on very slowly. Should it not be strong enough pour the water on again.

CHOCOLATE.
MRS. F. G. SLACK.

To 1 quart of milk take 2 squares of Whitman's best chocolate. Cut up fine and dissolve with a little warm water. When the milk is boiling put in the chocolate and stir almost constantly. It is better to use a chocolate-pot, containing a *muddler* which can be easily twirled between the hands, causing it to foam.

COFFEE.
MRS. PUTNAM, FROM MRS. BLISS.

With a little cold water mix one cup of freshly browned ground coffee—Java and Mocha mixed in equal parts. Put it into the coffee-pot, pour on it seven cupsful of boiling water, close the lid immediately and place over a hot fire. As soon as the coffee comes to a boil, pour out rapidly one cupful and return it immediately, close the lid and wait for the coffee to boil up again, then pour out another cupful and return it at once. Repeat the process the third time, then remove to a place on the fire sufficiently hot to keep the coffee scalding. It must not boil again. In twenty minutes it will be ready to serve.

MOCK CREAM FOR COFFEE.
MRS. DOUGLAS PUTNAM.

Heat a quart of *new* milk. Work together a dessertspoonful of sweet butter, with a teaspoon of flour, thinning it with a little of the hot milk. Add the mixture to the milk and beat it constantly for five minutes while boiling; then remove it from the fire and continue to beat it for five minutes longer. Have ready, well beaten, very light, the yolks of two fresh eggs, and add them to the cream while hot, mix well, strain through a fine sieve, and afterwards beat it until very light.

PROPORTION OF COFFEE TO WATER.

MRS. G. M. WOODBRIDGE.

In making only 1 quart of coffee use 4 heaping tablespoonsful of ground coffee to 1 quart of water. If making a quantity, take 3 heaping tablespoonsful to 1 quart of water. 1 quart of coffee will make 6 ordinary cups as full as necessary.

CHERRY SHRUB.

Boil the cherries till tender, strain out the juice and to each quart put 1 pint sugar. Cook 15 minutes, bottle and seal the corks with wax. Put a tablespoonful of this syrup in a tumbler, fill up with ice water, and you have a delicious beverage in hot weather.

DOMESTIC GINGER BEER.

Put 2 gallons of cold water on the fire, add to it 2 ounces of ginger and 2 pounds of sugar. Let this boil a half hour, skim the liquor and pour it into a jar with 1 sliced lemon and ½ ounce cream tartar. When nearly cold put into it a teacupful of yeast to cause it to work. When it has worked 2 days, strain it into bottles and cork tight. Tie the corks down firmly.

LEMONADE.

MRS. HORACE NORTON.

Three lemons to a quart of water, 6 tablespoons of sugar. Put the sugar in a pitcher, pour the lemon-juice on sugar, cut a part of lemons in slices and put with the juice and sugar, stir well and pour on water and pounded ice.

MEAD.

MRS. ROSSETER.

Three pounds brown sugar, 3 pints boiling water, 1 pint molasses, ¼ pound tartaric acid, 1 ounce essence wintergreen or sassafras, mix the ingredients and pour the boiling water on. Let it stand till cold and bottle, cork tight and put in cool place. Put 2 tablespoonsful in a tumbler, nearly fill with water, stir in a third of a teaspoonful soda. A delicious drink in hot weather. Will keep good a year.

RASPBERRY VINEGAR.

MRS. F. G. SLACK.

Put 4 pounds very ripe raspberries into 3 quarts of the best vinegar, and let them stand 3 or 4 days. Strain the vinegar through a jelly bag and pour it on the same quantity of fruit. Repeat the process in three days a third time. To each pound of the liquor thus obtained add 1 pound of fine sugar. Bottle it, and let stand covered but not tightly corked a week. Then cork tight and keep in cellar. Add water to it when you drink it.

TEA.

Two teaspoons of tea to one coffee cup of boiling water. Scald the tea pot well; put in the tea and covering close, set it on the stove one minute to warm. Pour on enough boiling water to cover and let it stand ten minutes to draw. Do not let it boil. Fill with as much boiling water as you need, and send hot to the table. Boiling after the tea is made, injures the flavor, making it rank and "herby."

BLACK TEA.

MRS. GEO. DANA.

An earthen tea pot, that can be easily cleansed, well scalded. Boiling water (fresh). A teaspoon of tea to a person. Steep but not boil ten minutes.

EGG LEMONADE.

PHILADELPHIA PRESS.

Break an egg into a tumbler. Rub two lumps of sugar on the rind of a fine lemon. Put the sugar into the tumbler, squeeze the lemon in with the squeezer, half fill the tumbler with fine ice, fill up with water and with a shaker, shake the whole vigorously for a few seconds, then grate a little nutmeg over the top. If you have no shaker beat the egg with a fork.

SYRUP FOR BEVERAGES.

Pour a pint of boiling water on a pint of sugar. When dissolved bottle for use. The use of syrup prevents the last of a cup being too sweet.

PICKLES, CATSUPS, ETC.

" Old-fashioned but choicely good."

Vinegar to keep pickles should be at least two years old.

BORDEAUX SAUCE.
MRS. ISRAEL WATERS.

Two gallons chopped cabbage, 1 gallon chopped green tomatoes (drain the juice off), 1 dozen onions chopped, 1¾ pound sugar, 1 ounce each, celery seed, black pepper, alspice, cloves—whole, ½ pound white mustard seed, 1 gill salt, 1 gallon vinegar—mix, boil 20 minutes.

CUCUMBER CATSUP.
MRS. TUPPER NYE.

Three dozen white cucumbers, 8 white onions, peel and chop as fine as possible, sprinkle over ¾ pint salt and put in a sieve to drain, then add 1 teacup ground pepper, mix and put in a jar covering with vinegar. After standing 24 hours pour off the vinegar, pour on more vinegar and seal closely in quart bottles.

RIPE TOMATO CATSUP.
MISS BARBER.

Three gallons of peeled tomatos, boiled slowly until they will rub through a sieve, add 1 quart of vinegar, 6 tablespoons salt, 1 tablespoon ground allspice, 6 tablespoons mustard, 2 tablespoons black pepper, 1 tablespoon cloves, ½ tablespoon mace, ½ tablespoon red pepper.

TOMATO CATSUP.
MRS. M. L. GODDARD.

After boiling and rubbing the tomatos through a sieve—to every gallon of the juice thus obtained measure out 4 tablespoonsful of salt, 4 tablespoonsful ground pepper, 2 tablespoonsful of allspice, 8 tablespoonsful of mustard, 4 pods of red pepper. Boil away the tomato juice half. When cold add the spices, except the red pepper, which boil with the tomatos. Add no more vinegar than necessary to bottle it. Fill the neck of the bottle with vinegar, cork and seal. Thin with vinegar when put on the table—will keep years.

TOMATO CATSUP.

MRS. FRAZYER.

Five quarts of ripe tomatos cooked as for use. Strain through a sieve 2 tablespoons of salt, 2 tablespoons of pepper, 1½ tablespoons of ground mustard, ½ tablespoons allspice, ½ tablespoons cloves, 4 ripe peppers ground fine, 1½ pints of vinegar. Simmer the whole four hours, then bottle ready for use and set in a cool place.

TOMATO CATSUP — Excellent.

MRS. LUTHER EDGERTON.

Boil and rub your tomatos through a sieve. To every gallon of the juice add 4 tablespoons of salt, 4 tablespoons of ground black pepper, 2 tablespoons of allspice, 3 tablespoons of mustard, 8 pods of red pepper. Boil the juice half away. When cold add the spices—except the red peppers, which boil with the tomatos.

GREEN TOMATO CATSUP.

One peck tomatos chopped fine, drain an hour, then put them in a vessel and cover with water and boil tender, then drain half an hour, chop 6 green peppers and mix. Take 2 quarts of vinegar and 1 pound of sugar, 1 teacup of salt, 1 teaspoonful of black pepper, cloves and cinnamon. Boil the ingredients in the vinegar and pour on the tomatos hot.

MRS. GEO. DANA'S CURRANT CATSUP.

Five pounds of fruit, 4 pounds of sugar boiled together about 2 hours. Then add spices, 1 tablespoon of each, cinnamon, cloves, allspice, 1 pint of vinegar. Boil this 15 or 20 minutes longer. Bottle it while hot. Do not let it thicken too much, so that it can not be poured from the bottle.

GOOSEBERRY CATSUP.

Eight quarts gooseberries, 4 pounds sugar, 1 pint vinegar, 2 ounces cloves, 2 ounces cinnamon. Boil slowly 4 hours. Tie the spices in a bag, and add the last half hour.

TOMATO CHOW-CHOW.

MRS. DANIEL TORPY.

To ½ bushel green tomatos take 12 onions chopped fine, sprinkle 1 pint of salt over this and let it stand over night. Then drain well and cook this in weak vinegar slowly for 1 hour. Drain off this vinegar, and take 2 heads of cabbage chopped fine and stir this in with 1 ounce of celery seed, 2 tablespoonsful of cinnamon, 1 of mustard seed and 1 of allspice, and 1 pint of horseradish chopped fine, and 2 pounds of sugar. Mix well together and pack in a jar. Vinegar sufficient to make it a little thin and to keep well. Pour this over the tomatos, onion, cabbage, spices, etc., in the jar, and it is ready for use.

OLD VIRGINIA CHOW-CHOW.

MRS. BETTY WASHINGTON LOVELL.

One-half peck of green tomatoes, 2 or 3 large heads of cabbage, 25 large cucumbers, 1 pint of grated horseradish, ½ pound of white mustard seed, 1 ounce of celery seed, ½ teacup tumeric and cinnamon, some small silver onions. Cut the tomatos, cabbage, cucumbers and onions fine, and salt them over night. In the morning drain off the brine and put them to soak for a day or two in vinegar and water. Drain this off. Then mix in the spices. Boil 2 gallons of vinegar with 4 pounds of sugar and pour on. Pour this off and heat it up for 3 mornings. The third morning mix 1 pound of flour of mustard with 1 pint salad oil, and mix in with it.

CHILI SAUCE.

MRS. DROWN.

Eighteen ripe tomatoes, 1 onion, 3 green peppers, 1 cup of sugar, 2 teaspoonsful of salt, 1 teaspoonful of each kind of spice, 2½ cups of vinegar. Cook for 3 hours, bottle it like catsup.

AN OLD RECIPE FOR PICKLES.

MRS. H. P. WHITNEY.

Make a brine not too strong and pour scalding hot over the cucumbers every day for a week taking off the scum which will rise. After that put them in a brass kettle with equal parts of water and vinegar and a piece of alum as large as a hickory nut pulverized. Stir occasionally until scorching hot, then set them off to cool, stirring occasionally. Drain off and put in a jar pouring hot vinegar over, then adding pepper, mustard seed and horse radish. If cloves are used, put them in a muslin bag, ground.

PICKLED CORN.

KATY RICE.

Boil on ear, then cut off. To 3 pints of corn add one of salt, mix well, when cold press down in the jar, once in a while wipe off the scum from the corn and sides of the jar and the plate. To use it soak over night. In the morning change water, set on the stove and heat gradually and then change again, then cook adding a spoonful of sugar.

OUDE.

MRS. GEO. EUSTIS.

1 peck green tomatos, 8 small green peppers, 1 cup salt, 1 cup sugar, 1 cup chopped nasturtions, 1 tablespoon ground cloves, 1 of allspice, 1 of cinnamon, 1 of mustard. Sprinkle the salt over the tomatos after they are sliced and let stand over night. Pour off water in morning, add the other ingredients, put into a kettle and boil 6 or 8 hours. Some add four onions.

CABBAGE PICKLE.

MRS. SLACK.

Three large cabbage heads, 6 green peppers chopped fine, ½ pint of mustard seed, 1½ pints of horse radish grated, 1 cup of sugar, ½ cup of salt. Mix well and cover with cold vinegar. It will be ready for use in three days.

CHERRY PICKLE.

MRS. WHEELER, KENTUCKY.

Take fresh cherries, (not too ripe) leave the stems on, and place them in a glass jar as compact as you can without bruising them. To 1 quart of cider vinegar, put 1 teacup of sugar and a tablespoonful of salt. When it is dissolved pour it over the cherries and fasten them up to keep air-tight. Keep them in the dark and cover the jars to preserve the color. Grapes can be made the same way.

PICKLES.

MRS. CHARLES SHIPMAN.

One gallon of vinegar, 1 cup of sugar, 3 dozen black peppers, 3 dozen cloves, 1½ dozen allspice, mace, red pepper, mustard seed. Boil 5 minutes.

CUCUMBER PICKLES.

MRS. DROWN.

Wash cucumbers and put in brine 24 hours. Take them out, wipe dry and lay in a jar, pour cold vinegar over them and let stand 5 or 6 weeks; then remove from vinegar and lay in jar, sprinkling some mixed spices between the layers of cucumbers, put on top a cup of sugar, pour over this hot vinegar in which a little alum has been dissolved. Keep the pickles under the vinegar by pressing a plate over them. Tie up the jar and they will keep a year.

CUCUMBER PICKLES.

MRS. A. J. WARNER.

Take small, green cucumbers, cover them with a weak brine, and let them stand 24 hours. Then take out the cucumbers, and wipe the black specks from them. Put them into a brass kettle, add sufficient vinegar to cover them, and a small lump of alum. Heat slowly, stirring them from the bottom occasionally. When scalded, turn them into a crock and let them stand 24 hours. Add a few green peppers, sliced.

To 600 pickles, take 3 gallons vinegar (if needed to cover them), 3 pints brown sugar, 3 gills of mustard seed, a large handful of cloves, a handful of cinnamon, 1 teaspoonful of celery seed, a few pieces of ginger-root, and a lump of alum the size of a walnut. Tie all the spices in a muslin bag and scald with the vinegar in a porcelain kettle. Drain the first vinegar from the cucumbers, and pour over them the spiced vinegar after it has cooled a little. Add some green grapes and horse radish, when cold.

CUCUMBER.

MRS. HAWKS.

Wash the cucumbers clean. Make a brine and pour scalding hot over them. Let stand 3 hours. To 1 gallon of vinegar add 1 piece of alum, size of a hickory nut. Let it get scalding hot. Put your pickles in and let them remain 15 minutes. Then take them out, and throw the vinegar away. Now take 1 gallon of fresh vinegar and add to it 1 green pepper cut in two. Cinnamon and cloves, if you like, and a little alum. Let this also come to a scald. Put the pickles in and let them scald. Seal up in glass jars. Be sure and get good apple vinegar and your pickles will keep.

CHOPPED PICKLE.

Four heads of cabbage, ½ bushel cucumber, ¼ bushel onions, 1 ounce each of nutmeg, cinnamon, cloves, mace, celery seed, mustard, cayenne pepper, tumeric, 2½ pounds white mustard seed. Scald the 2½ pounds white mustard seed in salt and water and let stand in the water over night. In the morning drain and put near the fire to dry. Chop the onions, cabbage and cucumbers very fine, sprinkle salt through them and put each into a jar by itself and stand till night, when put each in a bag by itself to drain till morning. Then mix the three together and add the spices and 3 pounds sugar. Cold vinegar enough to mix them well. Put into jars and cover with vinegar, let stand 24 hours and cover again with vinegar, then tie up for use.

FRENCH PICKLES.

MRS. RUTHERFORD B. HAYES.

One peck of green tomatos sliced, 6 large onions sliced, mix, and throw over them a teacup of salt, and let them stand a night. Next day drain, and boil in 1 quart vinegar and 2 quarts water for 15 minutes, then drain. Take 4 quarts vinegar, 2 pounds brown sugar, ½ pound white mustard seed, 2 tablespoons of ground allspice, cinnamon, cloves, ginger and ground mustard, throw all together and boil 15 minutes.

GREEN TOMATO SOY.

MRS. NAHUM WARD.

One peck of green tomatos sliced, add half a pint of salt and let it stand 24 hours. Then drain and put in a preserving kettle with 1 dozen onions sliced, 1 ounce of black pepper, 1 ounce of allspice, ¼ pound of ground mustard, ½ pint of mustard seed. Cover with vinegar and boil until thick as jam or about 2 hours.

GREEN TOMATO PICKLE.

MRS. NAHUM WARD.

Slice or chop 1 gallon of green tomatos and salt over night. In the morning mix 1 tablespoonful ground black pepper, 1 of mace, 1 of cloves, 4 pods red pepper chopped fine, ½ pint grated horseradish, mix thoroughly, put in a jar and cover with cold vinegar, onions to taste.

GREEN TOMATO PICKLE.

MRS. FRANCES NYE STURGES.

One peck of green tomatos sliced, 1 dozen onions sliced, sprinkle with salt and let stand until next day to drain. They may be drained by tying in a large cloth and then hung up. The next day add 1 box of ground mustard, 1½ ounce of black pepper, 1 ounce of mustard seed, 1 ounce of allspice, ½ ounce of whole cloves. Put in a kettle, layer of tomatos and onions alternating. Sprinkle over the spice. Put the mustard in the vinegar and put on vinegar enough to cover the whole. Let it boil 20 minutes.

GERMAN PICKLES.

MRS. D. E. BEACH.

Two hundred small cucumbers laid in brine for 24 hours. Bay leaves, dill seed, mustard seed, grated horse radish. Put the cucumbers in a jar with the leaves, and seeds, and horse radish in alternate layers. Boil 1 quart of vinegar, with 1½ cups of sugar, and pour on hot. Cover the pickles and seal the jars while hot.

MRS. GEORGE DANA'S GRAPE PICKLE.

Seven pounds of grapes, 3 pounds of sugar, 1 pint of vinegar. Pulp the grapes. Cook the skins in the vinegar and sugar, cook the pulps in a little water. Strain them in a sieve, and when the skins are cooked, add the strained pulp and let it boil once. Then all is done.

TO PICKLE MARTINOS.

MRS F. G. SLACK.

Gather the martinos while young and tender, put them in a strong brine till ready to pickle, changing the brine once during the time. Put them in weak vinegar 24 hours; take them out of the vinegar and put them in a jar with a good deal of horse radish, black and red pepper, allspice, race ginger, a few cloves, a tablespoonful of celery seed and a little garlic if you like. To every gallon of the vinegar put ¾ pound of brown sugar, scalding it in the vinegar and pour over the martinos while boiling.

PEPPER PICKLES — Excellent.

MRS. BLISS.

Pick the peppers late in the season before they begin to turn red, soak them 10 days in a strong brine of salt and water, then if they have a good green color, remove them from the brine to clear cold water, in which let them stand 24 hours. If they have not a good green color, they will get it by scalding in the brine. Drain them, remove the seed, scraping them out through a slit cut in the side of each pepper. Fill them with red or white cabbage, cut very fine, pour boiling vinegar over them, sufficient to cover all, when cool, pack in jars. After filling each pepper, the slit should be sewed up.

PICKLED PLUMS.

MRS. M. B. HASKELL.

One peck of plums, 7 pounds of sugar, a pint of good vinegar and spices to taste. Boil till well cooked. Nice with meats.

PEACH MANGOES.

Wash off the fuzz off the peaches, cut them in half, fill them with white mustard, a few cloves, mace and cinnamon. Tie them up and put them in a jar, and pour over them three mornings, boiling vinegar sweetened to taste.

SPICED TOMATOS.

MRS. M. B. HASKELL.

Take ripe tomatos, peel and slice them. To 1 quart tomatos take 1 pint vinegar and 1 pint sugar, of which make a syrup and pour over the fruit. Next morning strain off the syrup, heat, and pour over again. The third morning pour all together into a kettle, add spices (unground) and boil slowly 1 hour, or till quite thick.

TO MAKE ANY KIND OF SWEET PICKLE.

MRS. SLACK.

Seven pounds fruit, 4 pounds sugar, 1 pint vinegar. Boil sugar and vinegar together 7 or 8 mornings and pour over the fruit. Have your spices in a lace bag and boil every day in the vinegar. The last morning boil the fruit in the vinegar, a *good while*, until it is clear.

SWEET TOMATO PICKLE.

To 7 pounds of tomatos add 4 pounds of sugar and boil until the sugar penetrates the tomatos. Then add 1 pint of vinegar, 1 ounce of cloves, 1 ounce of ground cinnamon, and boil a half hour.

SPANISH PICKLE.

MRS. EDGERTON.

Cucumbers full grown pared and quartered lengthwise, cut all into pieces about half an inch thick. For a layer of the cucumber pieces use about as much salt as is used for cucumber catsup. Let it stand in the salt 1 night, then drain thoroughly. Vinegar 1 gallon, of cloves, race ginger, white mustard seed, celery seed, 2 ounces each, mustard 2 large boxes mixed in vinegar, brown sugar 1 pound, turmeric 1 ounce put into the vinegar, horseradish sliced and red peppers to your taste. Boil this and pour over the cucumbers.

YELLOW PICKLE.

MRS. GEO. M. WOODBRIDGE.

One-half pound ginger sliced, ½ pound horseradish scraped, 1 ounce garlic (or 1 dozen onions) sliced and salted, ½ pound white mustard seed, 1 ounce mace, 1 ounce nutmeg, 1 ounce small long peppers, 2 ounce of turmeric, 2 pounds of brown sugar, 2 gallons vinegar, 2 dozen heads early York cabbage cut in quarters. Scald the vegetables in brine strong enough to float an egg. Let them remain 2 days then squeeze them well in a towel and put them in a jar, with cold vinegar sufficient to cover them, well colored with perhaps an ounce of turmeric, let them remain 2 weeks. Then place them with the 2 gallons of vinegar, the spices and sugar named, in a bright kettle over a clear fire. Boil 15 or 20 minutes. Pour into a jar and tie up immediately with leather or enameled cloth.

SPICED CURRANTS.

(TO BE EATEN WITH MEATS.)

MRS. DOUGLAS PUTNAM.

Five pounds currants, 4 pounds of brown sugar, 1 pint of vinegar, 1 tablespoonful of ground cloves, 1 tablespoonful of cinnamon, 1 tablespoonful allspice (all tied up in a thin bag). Boil 50 minutes. Dissolve sugar in vinegar, heat, then add fruit.

Salads, Salad Dressings, Oysters, Etc.

"TO MAKE IT ONE MUST HAVE A SPARK OF GENIUS."

"My salad days,
When I was green in judgment."
—*Shakespeare.*

BAKED SALMON.

MRS. DIMMICK, SCRANTON, PA.

Boil 6 pounds of lake salmon. Boil it, in the cans, 20 minutes, then open the can, and pour off the oil. When cold, pick it to pieces. Make a sauce of 1 quart of rich milk in which boil 1 onion, cut up and tied in a bag. Rub 5 tablespoons of flour in 1 cup of butter. Stir into the milk when it boils. Season with red pepper, salt, and chopped parsley. When cold put the fish and the sauce in layers in baking dish. Sprinkle the top with bread or cracker crumbs. Bake until a light brown.

MRS. A. B. WATERS'S BEEF LOAF.

Three and one-half pounds of chopped beef, 3 eggs, butter size of an egg, ¾ tablespoon pepper, 1 tablespoon salt, ½ nutmeg, 4 tablespoons cream (in winter), 6 or 8 soda crackers.

CHICKEN SALAD.

MRS. H. TOWNE, PORTSMOUTH.

Four chickens, 8 bunches celery, 8 eggs (yolks only) well beaten, 1 tablespoon sugar, 1 tablespoon salt, 2 tablespoonsful prepared mustard, a little cayenne pepper, ½ cup sweet cream, 1 pint of vinegar, 1 cup of butter or olive oil. Boil together, stirring constantly, and pour over chicken and celery.

CHICKEN SALAD.

MRS. MELLISSA S. NORTHROP, BELPRE.

Four eggs, 1 chicken, 1 teaspoon salt, 1 teaspoon of common pepper, 1½ gills of table mustard, 1½ wine glass of vinegar, 2 wine glasses of sweet oil, 2 heads of celery.

CHICKEN SALAD.

MRS. ARIUS NYE, BROOKLYN.

The white meat and second joints of three boiled chickens cut moderately fine, 3 large heads of celery, 12 hard-boiled eggs. Bruise the yolks to a paste with 9 tablespoons of salad oil, 3 ounces of melted butter, 9 teaspoons of salt, a pint and a half of sharp vinegar, 9 teaspoons of mixed mustard. Chop the whites of the eggs and cut the celery. Set all the ingredients in a cool place and mix thoroughly just before serving. Chopped cabbage may be substituted for the celery. If used, flavor with celery salt.

CHICKEN SALAD.

MRS. WM. NYE.

Take 2 large fowls, cold, the yolks of 9 eggs, hard-boiled, ½ pint of butter, ½ pint of vinegar, 2 large heads of celery, chop and mix well. Season with Durkie's salad dressing. It is improved by adding some chopped cucumber pickles.

CHICKEN CROQUETTES.

MRS. WOODRUFF.

Chop the meat of one chicken fine, also add ½ of a middling sized onion, fry the onion with 1 ounce of butter, add 1 teaspoonful of flour, stir half a minute, then add the chopped meat and a little over a gill of the broth, salt, pepper and a pinch of nutmeg, stir for about 2 minutes, take from the fire, mix the yolks of 2 eggs with it, put it back on the fire for 1 minute, stirring the while, turn into a dish to cool, when perfectly cold mix well, roll into the shape you want, then roll in bread or cracker crumbs, then in egg and again in cracker crumbs. Fry in hot lard—use veal if you prefer.

CHICKEN CROQUETTES.

MRS. PARLOA.

One solid pint of finely chopped cooked chicken, 1 tablespoon of salt, ½ teaspoon of pepper, 1 teacup of cream or chicken stock, 1 tablespoon of flour, 4 eggs, 1 teaspoon of chopped parsley, 1 teaspoon of onion juice, 1 tablespoon of lemon juice, 1 pint of bread crumbs, 3 tablespoons of butter. Put the cream or stock on to boil, mix flour and butter and stir in, add chicken and seasoning. Boil two minutes and add two of the eggs well beaten and set away to cool. When cold shape and fry.

CABBAGE DRESSING.

For one head of cabbage take one coffee cup of cream, sweet or sour, one tea cup of vinegar, a large spoonful of sugar, a large spoonful of butter, teaspoon of salt, ½ teaspoon mustard, ½ teaspoon corn starch, pepper to taste. Heat until it boils, then pour over chopped cabbage, stirring all the time.

CABBAGE DRESSING.

MRS. S. MILLS ELLSTON.

One heaping teaspoon of mustard, 1 heaping teaspoon of salt, 2 heaping teaspoons of cream, 1 heaping teaspoon of butter, 3 heaping teaspoons of sugar, yolks of 2 eggs, ⅔ of a cup of vinegar.

CABBAGE DRESSING.

MRS. BEMAN GATES.

One teacup of vinegar, made hot, (not boiling) the yolks of 2 eggs, beaten and stirred in after it is taken off from the fire, add 2 tablespoons of sugar, 1 teaspoon of mustard and butter the size of a hickory nut, and half a cup of cream.

CREAM FISH.

FOURTH STREET COOKING CLUB.

Pick in pieces 2 pounds of canned salmon. For sauce: ½ quart of milk in which boil a little onion cut up and tied in a bag. Rub 2 tablespoons of flour in ½ cup of butter, stir into milk, when it boils season with salt, black pepper, parsley. Put fish and sauce into a baking dish in alternate layers. Cover the top with bread crumbs and bake brown.

CELERY SALAD.

BREVOORT HOUSE.

Cut up celery into small pieces and pour over it mayonnaise dressing.

ESCALOPED SALMON.

ELIZABETH ANDERSON.

Pick the bones from canned salmon. Place in a buttered baking dish a layer of bread crumbs, a layer of salmon with butter, pepper and salt, finishing with crumbs, on which lay bits of butter. Add the liquor from the salmon and milk, or milk and water—half

Salads, Salad Dressing, Oysters, Etc.

as much more as would be required for the same bulk of oysters. Bake one hour.

HAM PATTIES.

MRS. ROSSETER.

Chop fine some scraps of lean ham. Mix with this a good deal of crumbed bread. Season with pepper. If the ham is all lean a lump of butter. Moisten with milk to a soft paste. Fill your muffin tins with this and break an egg upon the top of each. Sprinkle pepper and salt on this and a few cracker crumbs and bake until the egg is done. Takes about 10 minutes.

HAM FOR SANDWICHES.

One pint of Chopped ham, 1 teaspoonful of mustard, 5 tablespoonsful of vinegar, 1 egg, pinch of salt.

JELLIED CHICKEN.

MRS. LUCY WOODBRIDGE SMITH.

Boil 3 chickens till tender, then skin them and cut the meat in small pieces. While the water they were boiled in is hot, skim off all of the grease. Take a quart of the remainder and pour it over one-half box of gelatine. Season with salt and pepper. Pour this over the chickens and set it in a cool place.

LETTUCE DRESSING.

MRS. SESSIONS, COLUMBUS, O.

One dessertspoonful of butter with a little flour rubbed into it. Take ⅔ of a teacup of vinegar and ⅓ of water, and let it just come to a boil, then stir into this the butter and flour. Add 1 teaspoon of sugar, 1 dessertspoon of ground mustard, a little cayenne and salt, and 1 egg, beaten lightly.

LOBSTER SALAD.

MRS. PILLSBURY.

Boil a large potato, mash it very fine. Mix the yolks of two eggs with the potato, until smooth. Stir into this 4 tablespoons of salt, 1 tablespoon of made mustard and a little pepper. Add to this the green fat of the lobster. Chop the lobster, reserving the claws to garnish. Take one large head of lettuce, lay the outer leaves on the dish.

Chop the rest of lettuce and add with the dressing to the lobster. Mix thoroughly, and when mixing add 1 cup of vinegar. Garnish the dish with two hard-boiled eggs, sliced and laid around with the claws.

MINT SAUCE.

MRS. LOVELL.

Two tablespoons of chopped mint, one tablespoon of sugar and a half tea cup of vinegar. Made an hour or two before serving.

MINT SAUCE.

MRS. HAWKS.

Chop or cut into small pieces a handful of mint, put 2 tablespoonsful of sugar on it. Have vinegar with nearly half water hot, and pour over the mint, cover and let stand a little while before using.

MAYONNAISE.

Yolks of 2 eggs beaten light, 1 teaspoon of salt, 1 teaspoon of sugar, 1 teaspoon of dry mustard, 1 tablespoon of olive oil or melted butter, a little pepper, 4 tablespoons of hot vinegar, which must be added slowly, beating all the time, stir until thick and light. It can be returned to the fire and stirred till it thickens, but must not boil. This is sufficient for 6 persons when you use lettuce, but not for salmon, lobster or chicken salad.

HOT SLAW.

Slice your cabbage fine and make a dressing of ½ cup of vinegar, ½ cup of cream, 1 egg, 1 tablespoon of butter, 1 teaspoon of salt, 1 tablespoon of sugar, pour on the slaw and set it on the stove in a covered kettle and let it come to a boil. Serve hot.

MAYONNAISE DRESSING.

The yolks of 3 eggs, a heaping teaspoonful of mustard, a teaspoonful of sugar, a little salt, a few drops of essence of celery. Stir gradually into this as much salad oil as you like, or if you prefer it, melted butter, and stir, and stir with a fork *ad libitum, ad infinitum*. Add 2 tablespoons of vinegar and a little cayenne pepper. It will be thick like jelly. When you use it, thin with vinegar to the consistency of cream.

MAYONNAISE DRESSING.

FOR SALADS, TOMATOS, ETC.

MRS. C. R. RHODES.

Break the yolk of a *fresh* egg on a plate and stir briskly round and round with a silver fork, adding very slowly olive oil, and ½ teaspoonful of salt. Consistency comes from the oil and salt. When the egg has absorbed a gill of oil, and is as stiff as mush, add slowly a little vinegar and a pinch of cayenne pepper.

STEWED OYSTERS.

Drain the liquor from 2 quarts of firm, plump oysters; mix with it a small teacupful of hot water, add a little salt and pepper, and set over the fire in a saucepan. When it comes to a boil, add a large cupful of rich milk (cream is better.) Let it boil up once, put in the oysters, let them boil for five minutes or less—not more. When they "ruffle," add 2 tablespoonsful of butter, and the instant it is melted and well stirred in, take the saucepan from the fire. Serve with oyster or cream crackers, as soon as possible. Oysters become tough and tasteless when cooked too much, or left to stand too long after they are withdrawn from the fire. A good and safe plan is, to heat the milk in a separate vessel set in another of hot water, and after it is mingled with the liquor and oysters, stir assiduously or it may "catch," as the cooks say—i. e., scorch on the sides or bottom of the saucepan.

OYSTER PIE.

MRS. DOUGLAS PUTNAM.

Cover a deep plate with rich puff paste and bake it, then fill with oysters, seasoned with a little salt, pepper, and plenty of butter, and 2 hard-boiled eggs sliced. Cover with just a sprinkling of cracker crumbs: over all pour the liquor from the oysters, and cover with puff paste, securing the edges well, and pricking the paste several times with a fork. Twenty minutes in a hot oven is required to bake it.

OYSTER PIE.

MRS. L. EDGERTON.

Spread rich paste around the edge and sides of a large deep dish. 100 oysters, 1 teaspoon salt, 1 teaspoon pepper, 1 tablespoon of nutmeg, cinnamon, and mace, mixed, 6 hard boiled eggs, chopped fine.

Pour oysters into the dish with as much liquor as you desire. Add seasoning, eggs and butter. Put on an upper crust, and bake in a quick oven.

OYSTER PIE.

DAPHNE.

Line a deep dish with puff paste. Put in oysters, seasoned with bits of butter, salt and pepper. Then pour on some of the oyster liquor and cover with the pie crust. Cut a hole in the top of crust, and bake thoroughly. It is well to sprinkle a little flour over the oysters.

OYSTER SAUCE FOR TURKEY.

MRS. M. L. OLDHAM.

One quart oysters. Put them on in thin liquor and let come to a boil. A heaping tablespoon of flour, rubbed into a half tea cup of butter. Add this to the oysters, stirring. At last add a tea cup of sweet cream.

FRICASSEED OYSTERS.

FOURTH STREET COOKING CLUB.

Let 1 quart of oysters and their liquor come to a boil. Pour off the liquor into a hot dish. Melt a piece of butter the size of an egg and stir into it, while on the stove a tablespoonful of flour, then a cupful of the oyster liquor. Take from the fire and mix in the beaten yolks of two eggs, a little salt, a very little cayenne pepper and one teaspoonful lemon juice. Heat this without letting it boil and put in the oysters. These may be served on slices of toast or in shells, or papers.

PICKLED OYSTERS.

MRS. ROSSETER.

Take fifty large oysters. Put in a stew pan and let come to a boil—no more. Take out of liquor, have ready one cup of vinegar in which has been boiled whole black pepper, nutmeg, salt and cloves to taste. Pour this over the oysters.

OYSTER SAUCE FOR CHICKEN OR SALMON.

MRS. ROSSETER.

Let a dozen or more oysters come to a boil in their own liquor. Mix a half cup of flour with ½ cupful melted butter, rub till smooth.

Put in a stew pan with the oyster liquor, adding salt, cayenne pepper, and a cup of sweet cream. Put on fire and let simmer till free from lumps. Just before taking from the fire add the oysters, cut in small pieces. Pour over fish on platter, but for chicken put in gravy boat.

OYSTERS ON TOAST.

MRS. H. C. EVANS.

Strain the liquor off of a quart of oysters. Put 1 cup of cream or rich milk and 1 cup of butter in the kettle. When this comes to a boil add 1 teaspoonful flour wet with a little cold water. Drop in the oysters. Let them boil up, adding salt and pepper. Lay slices of nicely toasted bread in a dish. Pour oysters over them and serve.

OYSTER CHOWDER.

MRS. RAMSEY.

Three-fourth pounds of pickled pork, 10 medium-sized potatoes, 6 small onions, 1 quart or can of oysters. Cut the pork into small pieces and fry in the kettle, chowder is to be prepared in. Next put in the onions and one quart of water, partly cook, then add the potatoes and another quart of water; when they are cooked enough put in a pint of milk and the oysters, season to taste and add crackers just before serving them.

OYSTERS WITH POTATOES.

MRS. RUTH M. HILL.

Line a good sized, round, deep dish with nicely mashed potatoes, have your potatoes rather stiff, build it up as high as you can at the edge, put into the oven to brown. When nicely browned take out and turn in two quarts of oysters, properly seasoned with butter, salt, and pepper. Stew in the fluid without water or milk. Slightly thicken with rolled crackers. Sprinkle a few cracker crumbs over the top. Brown to a rich color.

FRIED OYSTERS.

ELIZABETH ANDERSON.

Season rolled cracker with pepper and salt. Roll the undrained oysters in this, one at a time, covering them well. Fry in butter, being careful not to scorch. Do not cook too long, large oysters requiring only a few minutes after browning. Cook quickly and serve immediately. They should be plump and juicy.

FRIED OYSTERS.

MRS. PILLSBURY.

Take large oysters and lay on towel and dry, having cracker-meal ready, dip the oysters in meal, then in well-beaten egg, then in cracker meal, then fry in hot lard.

ESCALOPED OYSTERS.

MRS. F. G. SLACK.

Butter the bottom and sides of your baking dish. Then put in a thick layer of oysters, each of which has been examined carefully for pieces of shell; put lumps of butter thickly over the top, and pepper and salt. Then put on a layer, not too thick, of bread crumbs und pounded cracker, half and half. Add another layer of oysters, seasoning, bread and cracker crumbs, untill the dish is full, covering the top with the crumbs and with lumps of butter. There is no liquor of *any kind* to be added to this. If there has not been too large a proportion of bread and cracker used it will be moist enough—and will be *much better.* Bake at least one hour.

ESCALOPED OYSTERS.

MRS. PILLSBURY.

For one quart of oysters. Butter a pudding dish, then sprinkle a layer of bread crumbs, then put in a layer of oysters, then season with bits of butter, salt and pepper, then another layer of bread crumbs; moisten with equal quantities of milk and oyster liquor, repeat until dish is full, having crumbs on top. Place small bits of butter on top. Cover until nearly done, then remove cover and brown. Bake one-half hour.

OYSTER PATTIES.

Mix into a pint of grated green corn three tablespoonsful of milk one tablespoonful of flour, a piece of butter the size of a hickory nut, one teaspoonful of salt, half a teaspoonful of pepper, and one egg. Drop it by desertspoonsful into a little hot butter, and *saute* it on both sides. It resembles, and has much the flavor of fried oysters. It is a good tea or lunch dish. Serve it hot, on a warm platter.

POTATOES IN CROQUETTES.

Mash boiled potatoes through the colander. Mix 2 eggs, (1 at a time) with a quart bowl of the mashed potatoes, (peach blows are the best.) Spread flour on the board, make small rolls of the potatoes, beat 2 or more eggs, dip rolls of potatoes in egg, and then roll it in bread crumbs dried and powdered fine. Cook two or three moments in hot fat, turning them.

PATE DE VEAU.

MRS. DOUGLAS PUTNAM.

Three and one-half pounds finest part of leg of veal chopped very fine, 2 eggs, 1 tablespoonful of salt, 1 tablespoonful of pepper, 1 nutmeg, a slice of pork chopped fine. Work all together in the form of a loaf of bread, put bits of butter on top and grate over it crumbs of bread. Put into dripping pan with a little water, and baste often. Bake 2 hours. To be eaten cold cut in slices.

POTATO SALAD.

Four cold boiled potatoes, 2 hard-boiled eggs, chop fine together, 1 teaspoon of pepper, 1 teaspoon of mustard, 2 teaspoons of salt, 1 egg beaten light, 2 teaspoons of sweet cream, 4 teaspoons of good cider vinegar.

POTTED MEATS.

No way of preparing cold meats is so successful as potting. This process is in England an every-day affair for the cook. If there be ham, game, tongue, beef or fish on the table one day, you are quite sure to see it potted on the next day at lunch or breakfast. It is a very good way of managing left-over food, instead of invariably making it into hashes, stews, etc. These potted meats will keep a long time. They are not good unless thoroughly pounded, reduced to the smoothest possible paste, and free from any unbroken fiber.

Potted Ham.—Mince some cold cooked ham, mixing lean and fat together; pound in a mortar, seasoning at the same time with a little cayenne pepper, pounded mace and mustard. Put into a dish, and place in the oven half an hour; afterward pack it in potting-pots or little stone jars, which cover with a layer of clarified butter (lukewarm) and tie bladders or paste paper over them. This is convenient for sandwitches. The butter may be used again for basting meat or for making meatpies.

Potted Tongue (Warne).—Ingredients: One pound and a half of boiled tongue, six ounces of butter, a little cayenne, a small spoonful of pounded mace, nutmeg and cloves, each half a teaspoonful. The tongue must be unsmoked, boiled, and the skin taken off. Pound it in the mortar as fine as possible, with the spices. When perfectly pounded, and the spices are well blended with the meat, press it into small potting-pans; pour over the butter. A little roast veal, or the breasts of turkeys, chickens, etc., added to the tongue, are an improvement.

Potted Be.—This is well-cooked beef chopped and pounded with a little butter, pepper, salt and mace. Manage as for potted ham.

POTTED LIVER.
MRS. SLACK.

Boil a calf liver till tender. Chop very fine, season with salt and pepper and a little sage. Add a small piece of butter, mix well with three or four tablespoonsful of the liquor the liver was boiled in. Press down solid in pudding dish. Put over it a little of the liquor and set in oven twenty minutes.

PRESSED VEAL OR CHICKEN.
MRS. H. C. EVANS.

Four pounds of veal or two chickens, covered with water and stewed slowly till meat will drop from the bones, then chop. Let the liquor boil down to a cupfull. Put in a small cup of butter, 1 tablespoonful salt, 1 tablespoonful pepper, 1 egg, beaten, a little allspice. Stir through the meat and press.

PRESSED CHICKEN.
MRS. BEMAN GATES.

Boil the chicken till very tender. Take out the bones and gristle; remove the skin and fat. Boil the gravy down to 1 cupfull to a chicken. Add a little butter, season with pepper and salt. Add ½ cupfull of gelatine, dissolved in water. Pick, not chop the chicken, into small pieces. Heat thoroughly with gravy. Then pour into a pan and put a light weight upon it. Slice when cold.

RICE CROQUETTES.

Two cups of well-boiled rice, 1 tablespoon of melted butter, 2 beaten eggs, 1 tablespoon sugar, a little flour and salt. Roll in the flour and drop in boiling lard. Eat hot.

RUSSIAN SALAD.
MRS. DR. IDE.

One cup each of string beans, peas, beets, sweet potatoes, Irish potatoes, carrots, chopped pickles, and 2 stalks of celery, or one cup

Salads, Salad Dressing, Oysters, Etc.

of cabbage and celery seed. Canned beans and peas can be used. All of the vegetables must be cooked and then cut in ¼ inch cubes. When cold, mix with French dressing prepared as follows: 1 full pint of vinegar, 1 tablespoon of salt, 1 tablespoon of mustard, 1 teaspoon of pepper. Sufficient for a company of 25.

SYDNEY SMITH'S SALAD DRESSING.

Two boiled potatoes, strained through a kitchen sieve;
Softness, and smoothness to the salad give;
Of mordant mustard take a single spoon
Distrust the condiment that bites too soon;
Yet deem it not, thou man of taste, a fault,
To add a double quantity of salt.
Four times, the spoon with oil of Lucca crown
And twice with vinegar procured from town;
True taste requires it, and your poet begs
The pounded yellow of two well-boiled eggs.
Let onion's atoms lurk within the bowl, —
And (scarce suspected), animate the whole;
And lastly, in the favored compound toss
A magic spoonful of Anchovy sauce.
Oh, great and glorious! Oh, herbaceous meat!
'T would tempt the dying Anchorite to eat,
Back to the world he'd turn his weary soul
And plunge his fingers in the salad bowl.

SALAD DRESSING.
MRS. LYDIA PUTNAM.

Yolks of 8 eggs, 1½ teaspoonsful salt, 1½ sugar, 2 ground mustard, a pinch of cayenne pepper, 1 cup butter, 1½ cup sweet cream, 1 pint vinegar. Boil till it thickens.

SALAD DRESSING No. 2.

One heaping teaspoonful each of mustard, salt, and butter, 2 of cream, 3 of sugar, ⅔ cup of vinegar, 2 yolks of eggs, beaten. Put all together and set on the stove, stirring constantly until it thickens.

SALAD DRESSING.
MRS. H. W. LEONARD, CINCINNATI.

One-half pint of vinegar, ½ size of egg in butter, tablespoon of sugar. Boil this. Beat the yolks of four eggs or the whole of two with ½ cup cream. Add to the other two teaspoons of mustard, celery seed.

SLAW.

One-half head cabbage, cut fine; 1 large stalk of celery, cut fine, 1 hard-boiled egg, 2 ounces grated horseradish, 2 teaspoons mustard. Mix with vinegar, pepper and salt, to taste.

SALMON CROQUETTES.

MRS. PROF. MITCHELL.

Two cups salmon, well picked with a fork, 1 cup fine cracker crumbs, 1 cup cream; mix well and season with pepper, salt, and a *little* nutmeg. Roll in cracker crumbs, then in beaten egg, and again in cracker crumbs. Let them stand several hours before frying.

SALMON SALAD.

MRS. W. W. MILLS.

One can of salmon; remove all the bones and oil, and shred the salmon into small pieces. Take a little more celery than there is salmon, and cut it into small pieces, and mix it thoroughly with a fork. Use Sydney Smith's dressing.

SWEET BREAD CROQUETTES.

MRS. J. L. BLYMEYER.

Throw the sweet breads into cold water for an half hour, then cook until tender in salt water. Then throw them into cold water for a few minutes. Take out all the pipes and chop fine. To one pint chopped meat take ½ pint cracker crumbs or fine bread. One egg. Season to taste and mould into forms.

TO BOIL SWEET BREADS.

Boil in a little water till tender. Take from the water and gash well. Put butter, salt and pepper over them. Very delicate.

TO FRY AS CUTLETS.

Parboil after separating and removing stringy portions, then dip in beaten egg and cracker crumbs and fry as cutlets, or

Prepare and cut the size of a walnut, dip in egg and cracker crumbs, and fry as doughnuts, skimming out with skimmer.

Salads, Salad Dressing, Oysters, Etc.

TO STEW SWEET BREADS IN CREAM.
MRS. HICKOK.

Put 1 tablespoonful of butter and 1 tablespoonful of flour in a thick saucepan over the fire, and stir till smoothly blended. Have ready also ½ pint of milk, and ½ pint of cream, hot, and add this gradually to the buttered flour, till it is a smooth sauce, into which put the sweet breads, previously boiled, and cut into inch squares. Serve hot. (One may add nicely stewed and strained tomatos to the sauce.)

TO BROIL SWEET BREADS.

After blanching the sweet breads as above, cut in slices ½ an inch thick. Put between the bars of a buttered wire gridiron, and broil each side about 5 minutes, over hot coals. Season lightly with pepper, salt and butter. Serve hot.

TO FRY SWEET BREADS

Slice the sweet breads as for broiling. Season with pepper and salt. Dredge in a little flour. Have hot in the frying pan equal parts of butter and lard. Fry the sweet breads a light brown on both sides Remove to the platter. Make a thickening of 1 dessertspoon of flour, and 1 gill of water stirred into the fat in the pan. Season it and pour it over the sweet breads. Serve hot.

SWEET BREADS FOR INVALIDS.
MRS HICKOK.

Put the sweet breads (fresh from the market) into sufficient cold water to cover them well, adding 1 tablespoonful of salt to 1 quart of water. Let them lie in the salt water at least 1 hour, then place them over the fire, in more cold water, and salt, (adding other seasoning if you like, whole spices, pepper corns, parsley, bay leaves, lemon peel, onion, or any dried herb except sage. Do not confuse seasoning). Preserve them intact and use them successively. Then slowly bring them to the boiling point. This is called " Blanching " and must always be done. After boiling gently 15 minutes lay them again in cold water for 10 or 15 minutes. This will harden them, or make them more firm to cut, then trim them from all superfluous membrane and fleshy fibre. They can now be set away till wanted for use.

TURBOT.
MRS. JOHN EATON.

Six lbs. of fresh white fish, steam until tender, remove all bones and dark skin. Mince fine with fork. Season with salt and pepper.

DRESSING FOR TURBOT.

Boil 1 quart of milk, thicken it with flour to the consistency of cream seasoning with salt and pepper, ¼ lb. of butter, 2 eggs beaten light. When dressing is cool, add eggs. Place a layer of fish in a pudding dish and cover with dressing, sprinkling lightly with cracker crumbs rolled fine, repeating this till all fish is used. Sprinkle top with cracker crumbs. Bake ¾ of an hour. Sufficient for 12 people.

VEAL LOAF.

MRS. M. S. NORTHROP, BELPRE.

Three pounds of finely chopped veal (lean), 3 eggs (raw), 6 crackers, powdered, 2 tablespoons of milk or cream, 1 heaping tablespoon of salt, 1 tablespoon of thyme, 1 tablespoon of pepper. Mix all well together and form into a loaf. Put bit of butter on it, and baste often.

VEAL LOAF.

MRS. HORACE NORTON.

Three lbs. of veal, uncooked, 2 lbs. fresh pork, chopped fine, 8 or 10 crackers rolled fine, 2 tablespoons black pepper, 2 tablespoons salt, 1 tablespoon thyme, 2 bunches of parsley, 5 eggs. Mix all well together, pack firmly into an oblong loaf. Bake with water in the bottom of the pan, basting same as roast beef. Bake from 1½ to 2 hours according to the thickness of the loaf. Save some of the liquor the veal is boiled in for basting.

EGGS, OMELETTES, ETC.

*" The turnpike road to people's hearts I find lies through their mouths, or
I mistake mankind."*

A DELICATE WAY TO BOIL EGGS.

Have a pan of boiling water, put the eggs in and cover up closely, do not return it to the fire, but let it stand five minutes for those who like soft eggs and a minute or two longer for those who like them harder. The whites are more like poached eggs. The fresher the egg the longer it takes to cook.

TO BOIL EGGS.

Wash them before boiling. Let the water be boiling when you put them in and keep it boiling 3 minutes for very soft, in 4 minutes the yolk will be soft, 6 minutes will make it hard. Boil eggs 8 minutes for salads.

EGGS—BREADED.

Boil the eggs hard and cut in round thick slices. Dip each in beaten eggs well seasoned with pepper and salt, then in fine bread crumbs and fry in butter hissing hot. Drain off every drop of grease and serve hot.

EGG AU PLAT.

Two eggs, 2 tablespoons bread crumbs, 1 ounce butter, pepper, salt and a little nutmeg. Melt the butter in a small flat dish and sprinkle over 1 tablespoon of the bread crumbs. Break into this the eggs and sprinkle over the rest of the bread crumbs, also the pepper, salt and nutmeg. Bake in a quick oven five minutes.

OMELETTE.
ELIZABETH ANDERSON.

Three eggs beaten separately, ½ cup milk, 2 tablespoons corn-starch, a little salt, a small half teaspoonful baking powder. Mix quickly adding the whites last, and pour into a moderately hot skillet in which is plenty of butter. Cover and set on back of the stove as it scorches quickly. When done fold together and serve on hot platter.

OMELETTE.

MRS. WOODRUFF.

Four eggs beaten separately, ½ teacup sweet milk, 1 teaspoon flour, pepper and salt. Fry in butter.

OMELETTE.

MRS. DUDLEY WOODBRIDGE, DETROIT.

Beat the whites of 6 eggs to a stiff froth, seasoning as for omelette, and pour into a buttered baking pan. Pour on the froth (at equal distances) six tablespoons of cream. Then drop into each depression made by the cream, a yolk of egg, whole. Bake in good oven, and serve hot.

A VERY DELICATE OMELETTE.

MISS M. M. WOODBRIDGE.

Six eggs, the whites beaten to a stiff froth and the yolks well beaten. A teacup full of warm milk, with a tablespoonful of butter melted in it. A tablespoonful of flour, wet to a paste with a little of the milk, and poured to the milk. A teaspoon of salt an a little pepper. Mix all except the whites, add those last; bake immediately in a deep, round dish, or tin cake pan. Some like a little onion and parsley, chopped fine, and very fine chopped ham, or dried beef stirred through the omelette, before the whites of the eggs are added. Leave the omelette in the oven, till brought to the table in the pan it is baked in; it should be eaten immediately. Do not have the oven too hot and be careful that it does not bake too fast on top. It requires about 15 minutes to cook it thorough properly. Eat it with butter.

TO SCRAMBLE EGGS.

Have some butter in skillet, very hot. Season the eggs well, pepper and salt, and beat very light. Put into the melted butter and stir constantly till done—which will be as soon as they have become thick.

TO POACH EGGS.

Put a good deal of water in the skillet and let it be boiling. Break one egg at a time into the water; keep pouring the water with a spoon over the eggs till they are done. An egg poacher with rings, in which to place the eggs and keep them in shape, makes them look much nicer.

CHEESE STRAWS.

MISS E. L. NYE.

Two ounces butter, ¼ pound flour, rubbed together, 2 ounces grated cheese, yolks of two eggs, white of one. Mix well and roll them. Cut in strips half inch wide, four or five inches long and bake in a moderate oven about five minutes. Place on a plate in form of log cabin.

WELSH RABBIT.
MRS. S. WOODBRIDGE SCOTT, CHILLICOTHE.

Pour 2 cups of boiling milk over 1 cup of grated cheese and stir until dissolved and smooth. When cool add 3 eggs, well beaten, and a biscuit or small piece of bread crumbed up. Pour into a baking dish and bake a light brown.

CHEESE FONDU.
ANNIE G. RATHBURN.

Two cups sweet milk, 1 cup bread crumbs, 3 eggs, beaten very light, 1 tablespoonful melted butter, pepper and salt to taste. Soak the bread crumbs in the milk, adding a pinch of soda if it is not perfectly sweet; add the eggs, butter and seasoning, and lastly stir into the mixture a half pound of grated cheese. Butter a pudding dish and pour the fondu into it. Bake until it is slightly brown.

CAKES AND ICINGS.

"WHATEVER PLEASES THE PALATE NOURISHES."

"We can afford no more at such a price!"
—*Shakespeare.*

ANGEL'S FOOD.
MRS. MORRISON.

Whites of 11 eggs, 1½ tumbler of powdered sugar, sifted, 1 tumbler flour, 1 teaspoon vanilla, 1 teaspoonful cream of tartar. Beat eggs on a large platter. On the same platter add the sugar, then the flour which must be sifted 4 times, then measured, then add the cream of tartar and sift again. Add the vanilla last. Don't stop beating till you put it in the pan to bake, don't grease the pan. Bake 40 minutes in a moderate oven. Try with a straw and if too soft let it remain a few moments longer. Turn upside down and cool in the pan, when cold take it out and ice it. If the tube in the center of the pan is not higher than the sides, put something under the edge so it won't lie flat when turned over. The tumbler with which you measure should hold half a pint.

ANGEL'S FOOD.
MRS. REDDINGTON, WISCONSIN.

Whites of 10 eggs, 1½ tumbler sugar, 1 tumbler sifted flour, 1 heaping teaspoon cream of tartar. Beat the whites with a wire spoon till they are very stiff, add the sugar and beat it well, lastly stir in the flour and cream of tartar sifted together very lightly. Bake 40 minutes in a moderate and steady oven. If it is baked in a sheet it will not take so long.

CUSTARD ALMOND.

One half pint of sweet cream (small), yolks of 4 eggs, 3 or 4 tablespoons of sugar, 1 teaspoon (or a little more) of corn-starch dissolved in a little water. Beat yolks of eggs and sugar together and add the starch. When the cream boils stir it in and cook till sufficiently thick. Blanch ½ pound of almonds, chop ½ of almonds fine and stir into the cream, split the other ½ and lay on the icing.

FILLING FOR ALMOND CAKE.

MISS IRISH.

One cup thick sour cream, 1 cup powdered sugar, 1 lb. (in the shell) almonds blanched and chopped, the finer the better. Flavor with vanilla.

BRIDE'S CAKE.

MRS. EUNICE ANDERSON.

Three-fourth pound of butter, washed, to free from salt, and creamed, 1 pound loaf sugar, pounded and sifted, 1 pound flour, whites of 15 eggs. Flavor with lemon or rose water.

BLACK CAKE.

MISS MAME SLACK, KENTUCKY.

Mix 1 pound of butter, 1 pound sugar and 10 eggs, well together. Add 1 teacup of molasses, 1 pound of flour, 1 ounce cinnamon, 1 ounce cloves—beat well. Add 2 pounds raisins, 1 pound currant, ½ pound citron, 1 teacupful quince preserves, 1 teacupful raspberry preserves, 1 teacupful strawberry preserves, 1 teacupful blackberry preserves or jam, 1 pound orange preserves (optional). Roll the currants, raisins, and citron in flour to keep from sinking. Stir lightly. Bake 7 hours.

BERMUDA SPICE CAKE.

MRS. H. WHITNEY.

One-half pound brown sugar, ½ pound butter (a little less), 3 eggs, ½ cup sweet milk, ½ cup molasses, ¼ cup corn meal, 2½ cups flour, ½ pound raisins, ¼ pound currants. A little citron.

BRADLEY'S CAKE.

GRACE MAY THOMAS.

One cup sugar, ½ cup butter, 1 cup cold water, 5 eggs (whites), 3 cups flour, 3 teaspoonsful baking powder. Vanilla to taste. Bake in layers. Between layers put the ordinary icing and add English walnuts or any nuts, which may be preferred.

BACHELOR'S BUTTONS.

MRS. W. W. MILLS.

One-half teacup butter, 2 eggs, 3 small cups of flour, 2 cups powdered sugar. Rub the butter and flour together, then the sugar and moisten it with the eggs. Flavor with vanilla. Drop on tins, making large as macaroons. Very good.

These can be made twice the size of a macaroon. Add a pinch of preserve on each after baking; cover with icing.

CARAMEL CAKE.

MRS. DOUMONT.

Three cups of sugar, 1½ cups of butter, 1 cup of milk, 4½ cups prepared flour, 5 eggs.

CARAMEL FOR FILLING.

Three coffee cups of brown sugar, 1 coffee cup sweet milk, ½ coffee cup of butter. Stir gently while cooking. Cook till it will stiffen when cool. Spread (while warm) on the layers of cake. The cake should be baked in layers as for jelly cake. Cover the top with the same and set in an open sunny window to dry.

DAPHNE'S CREAM CAKES.

Four teacups of flour (or less), ¾ teacups of butter, 3 teacups of sugar, 5 eggs, 1 teacup sour cream, cinnamon, nutmeg. Bake in small pans. When partly baked sprinkle over several raisins and sifted sugar. Daphne always tried baking 1 or 2 cakes to tell the amount of flour needed, and seldom used quite 4 cups.

CREAM CAKES.

MRS. G. R. WOODRUFF.

Boil 1 cup butter in 1 pint of water, while boiling stir in 3 cups of flour, then take from the fire and stir in gradually 10 eggs till quite smooth. Do not beat them. Add ½ teaspoonful soda and drop on tin sheets the size you want them. Bake a half hour.

MIXTURE FOR FILLING.

Boil 1½ pint rich milk and stir into it while boiling 5 eggs, 2 cups sugar, 1 cup flour beaten together. Flavor to suit the taste. When cool remove the top of the cake and lay in some of the mixture.

FRENCH CREAM CAKE.

MRS. C. R. RHODES.

One teacup pulverized sugar, 3 eggs, 2 tablespoonsful cold water and put all together in a dish and beat light, 1½ cups flour, 2 tablespoons baking powder. Bake in 2 jelly cake pans. Split each cake and turn the cut side up, except the top one which must be sprinkled with fine sugar.

CREAM FOR FILLING.

One-half pint sweet milk, 1 tablespoonful common starch, 1 egg, all mixed and boiled till stiff as mush, then take from the fire and add ½ teacup sugar, 1 tablespoonful butter and 1 tablespoonful vanilla extract. Spread between the cakes.

CREAM SPONGE CAKE.

MRS. DROWN.

One cup of sugar, 1½ cups of flour, 3 eggs, 1 teaspoonful of cream of tartar, ½ teaspoonful soda. Bake in 3 layers.

CREAM.

One pint of milk, 2 eggs, 2 tablespoonsful of flour, 1 tablespoonful of corn starch, 1 cup of sugar.

CUP CAKE.

MRS. BEMAN GATES.

One cup of butter, 2 cups of sugar, 3 cups of flour, 4 eggs, ⅔ cup of milk, 1 teaspoon of baking powder.

COFFEE CAKE.

One cup of butter, 2 cups of brown sugar, 1 pound of raisins, 1 cup of molasses, 1 pound of currants, 1 cup of very strong coffee, citron, 1 egg, cloves, 4 or 5 cups of flour, baking powder.

COCOANUT CAKE.

MRS. H. B. SHIPMAN.

Beat 12 eggs, whites and yolks separately, mix together and add gradually 1 pound of sugar. Beat this 10 minutes, then stir in very lightly 1 pound of flour. It must not be beaten after the flour is in. Bake in jelly cake tins in a quick oven.

THE MIXTURE.—Soak ½ box of gelatine 1 hour, pour over ½ cup of warm water stirring till it is dissolved. Beat 1 pint rich cream to a froth, also the whites of 8 eggs. Grate 2 cocoanuts, stir the gelatine into the cream and add cocoanut and sugar enough to sweeten, 1 teaspoonful vanilla, then the whites of the eggs. Spread this between and on the top, also grated cocoanut on the top.

COCOANUT CONES.

MRS. WOODRUFF.

1 grated cocoanut, ½ pound powdered sugar, whites of 2 eggs, mix together, form in cones and bake on buttered paper.

CRULLERS.

MRS. JAMES HOLDEN.

Three eggs well beaten, 3 heaping tablespoons of pulverized sugar, 3 tablespoonsful of melted butter, nutmeg for flavoring, flour enough to roll conveniently. Fry in hot lard.

CUP CAKE.

MRS. WM. R. PUTNAM.

One and one-half cups of butter, 3 cups of sugar, 5 cups of flour, 6 eggs, 1 teaspoon of soda, 2 teaspoons of cream of tartar.

COOKIES.

MISS BARBER.

Two cups of sugar, 1 cup of butter, ½ cup of water, 2 eggs, 1 teaspoon soda.

COOKIES.

MISS BARBER.

One cup of butter, 2 cups of sugar, 3 eggs well beaten, 1 teaspoon of soda.

One teaspoon of nutmeg, ½ teaspoon of cloves, flour enough to make a soft dough, 2 cups or more.

MRS. GEORGE DANA'S COOKIES.

Two cups of sugar, 1 cup of butter, (or less if some cream is used,) ½ cup sour cream, 1 teaspoonsoda, flavor with lemon, flour to make just thick enough to roll out.

SPICE COOKIES.

MRS. ROSSETER.

One cup butter, 1 cup sugar, 1 pint molasses, 1 teaspoonful soda, 2 tablespoonsful ginger, 1 tablespoonful cloves, 2 tablespoonsful cinnamon. Flour to make stiff enough to roll.

Cakes and Icings.

VERY RICH COOKIES.

MRS. EUNICE ANDERSON.

One cup butter, 1 cup sugar, 1 beaten egg, nutmeg, enough flour to make a moderately stiff paste. Roll with as little kneading as possible.

SUGAR COOKIES.

CINCINNATI WOMAN'S EXCHANGE.

Two cups butter, 2½ cups sugar, 4 eggs, teaspoon soda. Flour to make stiff enough to roll.

COLORADO CREAM CAKE.

MRS. G. R. WOODRUFF.

One cup sour cream, 1 cup granulated sugar, 1 egg, ½ teaspoonful soda, dissolved in a spoonful hot water, 2 cups flour. Flavor. Stir them all together without beating the eggs separately.

DELMONICO FILLING.

MRS. W. G. WAY.

Two and one-half cups of light brown sugar, 1½ cup cream, 1 tablespoonful butter, 1 teaspoonful vanilla. Boil until it waxes in water. Spread while warm.

DETROIT SPICE CAKE.

MRS. D. B. WOODBRIDGE.

Three pounds seedless raisins, 1½ pound citron, 1 pound butter, 2½ cups sugar, 2 cups sweet milk, 4 cups flour, 6 eggs, 2 large teaspoons of baking powder, 3 teaspoons cinnamon, 2 teaspoons mace. Bake in loaves.

DOUGHNUTS.

MRS. DR. S. P. HILDRETH.

One pint of light dough, 3 eggs, 8 tablespoons melted butter, 8 tablespoons sugar, spice, 1 small teaspoon soda. Mix stiff and let them rise 5 hours. Mix again, roll out and fry them.

MRS. DR. S. P. HILDRETH'S HARD CAKES.

Three eggs, 1¼ cups butter, 2 cups brown sugar, 1 small teaspoon soda, 1 nutmeg. Flour enough to roll very thin.

DOUGHNUTS.

MRS. A. B. WATERS.

Four pints flour (or more, if needed, to make dough stiff), 4 eggs, 1 pint sugar, very fine; melt butter size of an egg, so that you can put it right in; 4 heaping teaspoons cream tartar, 2 level teaspoons soda, dissolve the soda in a little water, 1 small nutmeg, 1 pinch of salt. Beat the eggs well in a pint cup, then fill up the cup with sweet milk. Then stir with a large spoon till stiff enough to take up and work out into a soft dough. This can be set away and fried from day to day. Rolled in white sugar before frying.

MRS. SALA BOSWORTH'S DOUGHNUTS.

Four pints of flour, 4 teaspoonsful baking powder, 1 grated nutmeg, salt, 1 pint of sugar, 1 tablespoonful of butter. Beat up 4 eggs in a pint cup and fill it with sweet milk. Mix and knead well.

DOUGHNUTS.

MRS. BETTY WASHINGTON LOVELL.

Two pounds of flour, 1 cup of yeast, 2 pounds of sugar, 5 eggs, 1 quart of milk, ½ pound of butter. Warm the butter and milk together.

ELECTION CAKE.

MRS. JAMES HOLDEN.

One cup of sugar, 1 cup of yeast, 2 cups of milk, flour for a stiff dough, rise over night. In the morning add 1 cup of sugar, 1 cup of butter, 3 eggs, 2 cups of raisins. Mix not quite as stiff as bread. Put into pans, rise and bake.

FIG LAYER CAKE.

MRS. R. B. HART.

One cup of sugar, 3 *even* tablespoons of butter, 1 egg and yolks of 2, ¾ cup of milk, 2 cups of flour, 2 spoons baking powder. Bake in 3 layers.

FOR FILLING.

One cup of sugar, ¼ cup water. Boil until thick. When cool add white of 1 egg well beaten. Chop 8 figs fine and add the figs to sugar and egg, beat well and spread between the layers.

FIG CAKE.

MISS IRISH.

One and a half cup of sugar, whites of 5 eggs, small ¾ cup of butter, 2½ teaspoonsful baking powder, ½ cup milk, 2 cups flour. Bake in a sheet. Make boiled icing and put in 1 cup finely chopped figs.

COMMON FRUIT CAKE.

MRS. RHODES.

One large cup of butter, 2 of brown sugar, ½ cup Orleans molasses, 4 cups flour, ½ pint sweet milk, 8 eggs, 3 teaspoonsful baking powder, 3 teaspoonsful cinnamon, 1 teaspoonful cloves, 1 nutmeg, 3 teacups fruit. Bake 1½ hours.

FRUIT LAYER CAKE.

One-half cup of butter, 1 cup of sugar, 1½ cup of flour, ½ cup of rose water, 1 cup of raisins (chopped), 2 eggs, ½ teaspoonful soda. Bake in 3 layers, frosting or jelly between.

FRUIT CAKE.

MRS. W. B. MASON.

One pound sugar, ¾ pound butter, ½ pound flour, 8 eggs, 1 teacupful of sour cream, 1 teaspoonful of soda, or sweet milk and baking powder, 2 pounds raisins, 2 pounds currants, ½ pound citron, 1 nutmeg, 1 ounce cinnamon, 1 ounce spice, ½ ounce cloves. Bake two hours.

FRUIT CAKE.

MRS. H. C. VINCENT.

Two cups sugar, one cup sour milk, one cup butter, 3½ cups of flour, 3 eggs, 1 small teaspoonful soda, 1 pound raisins and spices.

MRS. BLIS'S POUND FRUIT CAKE.

MRS. L. E. PUTNAM.

Beat to a cream one pound of butter and one pound fine white sugar. Add the well beaten yolks of twelve eggs and beat the whole well together. Then add two glasses rose water, half an ounce of mace, powdered, and ½ pound sifted flour. Then mix in 1 pound stoned raisins, well dredged with flour, 1 pound currants, well washed, well dried and well dredged with flour, ½ pound citron, finely sliced and dredged. Beat the whites of the twelve eggs to a froth. To little over half a pound of flour add (well sifted through the flour) two teaspoonsful cream tartar, and stir the whites lightly into the flour. Add this to the other mixture. With one teaspoonful soda, well dissolved in hot water, two tablespoonsful. Bake as soon as the soda is mixed in, taking an hour and a half to two hours for baking. Cover with icing before the cake is cold.

FRUIT CAKE.

MRS. Z. D. WALTER.

One pound sugar, 1 pound butter, 1 pound flour, 2 pounds raisins, 2 pounds currants, ½ pound citron, 1 coffee cup brown sugar, 1 coffee cup molasses, with 1 teaspoonful soda, dissolved in it, 1 cup strong, clear coffee, 10 eggs beaten separately, 1 grated nutmeg, 1 dessertspoonful cinnamon, very little allspice. Wash and dry the currants, seed raisins, and chop half. Bake slowly 4 hours, with pan of water in the oven.

SOFT GINGER BREAD.

MRS. BETTY WASHINGTON LOVELL.

Six cups of flour, 3 teacups of molasses, 1 teacup of butter, 1 teacup of cream, 1 spoonful of soda (tablespoon,) ginger to your taste.

HARD GINGER CAKES.

CINCINNATI WOMAN'S EXCHANGE.

One pint of molasses, 6 dessertspoonsful of lard, 1 dessertspoonful of soda, 2 dessertspoonsful of ginger, 1 teaspoonful of salt, gill of tepid water, flour enough to roll and cut out.

GINGER BREAD.

REBECCA STONE.

One cup of sugar, 1 cup of molasses, 1 cup of cream, 3 cups of flour, 3 eggs, 1 teaspoon of ginger, 1 teaspoon of cinnamon, 1 teaspoon of salt.

GINGER BREAD.

MRS. KATHERINE WILKINS.

One cup of molasses, 1 cup of brown sugar, 1 cup of lard, 1 cup of sour milk, 2 eggs, 1 tablespoon of soda, 1 tablespoon of ginger, 1 teaspoon of cinnamon, 1 teaspoon of allspice, ½ teaspoon of cloves, 5 cups of flour. Good.

Cakes and Icings.

SOFT GINGER BREAD.
MRS. ARIUS NYE.

One cup of sour milk or buttermilk, 1 cup of shortening, 3 cups of molasses and 5 cups of flour, 1 *large* tablespoonful of ginger, 1 large teaspoon of soda, beat well.

GINGER BREAD.—Without Eggs.

One cup of butter, 1½ cups of molasses, 2 teaspoons of soda with 1 cup of boiling water poured over it, 1 tablespoonful of ginger, a little cinnamon, flour as needed—about 4 cups.

GINGER SNAPS.
MRS. DR. S. P. HILDRETH.

One tumbler of molasses, 2 tablespoons of butter, 1 teaspoon of soda, 1 tablespoon of ginger, flour enough to roll very thin.

GINGER SNAPS.
MRS. J. L. RECKARD.

Three-fourths of a cup of lard, 1 pint of molasses, 1 tablespoon each of ginger and soda, 1 teaspoon of mustard. Stir the soda, dissolved in a little warm water, in the molasses and mix with the melted lard, adding flour. Roll as thin as possible.

GINGER BREAD.
MRS. EDGERTON.

One cup of butter, 1 cup of molasses, 1 cup of sugar, 1 cup of sour milk or cream, 1 tablespoonful of ginger, 1 teaspoonful of cinnamon, 2 eggs and spice to your taste, 5 cups of flour, 1 teaspoonful of soda.

NANTASKET GINGER BREAD.
MRS. I. R. WATERS.

Two pounds of flour, 1 pound of sugar, ½ pound of butter, rub the butter and sugar to a cream and add 5 eggs, 2 tablespoons of ginger, 1 teaspoon of soda, then the flour. Roll very thin and cut in small cakes, and bake a light brown.

SOFT GINGER COOKIES.
MRS. EATON.

Two cups molasses, 11 tablespoons melted lard (or half butter), 9 tablespoons hot water, teaspoon salt, 3 teaspoons soda, dissolved in the molasses, tablespoon ginger. Flour enough to make very soft dough.

SOFT GINGER CAKES.

MRS. G. M. WOODBRIDGE.

One and a half tea cups molasses, 1 egg, ½ cup of butter or lard, ¾ cup of boiling water, 1 teaspoonful of soda, dissolved in the water, 3 cups (before it is sifted) of flour, 1 tablespoon ginger. If lard is used, add salt. Drop on buttered tins.

GOLD AND SILVER CAKE.

MRS. B. GATES.

One-half cup butter, 1 cup sugar, 2 cups flour, ½ cup milk, whites of 3 eggs. Repeat this for the Gold Cake, using the yellows of the eggs, and adding a little more milk.

Flavor the Silver Cake with almond. Flavor the Gold Cake with vanilla.

GERMAN BREAD.

MRS. BEACH.

Take enough of the light dough (ready for baking) for one loaf of bread. Add to it 1 small cup of sugar, 1 tablespoon of butter or lard, 1 cup of stoned raisins, spice to suit the taste, the beaten whites of 2 eggs. Knead well.

GRANDMA DUNN'S CAKE.

One cup of butter, 3 cups of sugar, 3 eggs, 1 teaspoon of soda, 1 cup of sour milk. Flour enough to make it stiff.

HARVARD CAKE.

MRS. HOLDEN.

One-half cup of butter, 2 cups of sugar, ¾ cup of milk, 3 eggs, 3 cups of flour, 1 small teaspoonful of soda, two of cream of tartar.

HERMIT COOKIES.

MRS. JOHN EATON.

Three eggs, 1½ cup of brown sugar, ½ cup of butter, 1 cup of currants, 1 teaspoon of soda, 1 teaspoon of cinnamon. Dissolve soda in a little milk. Flour enough to roll.

Cakes and Icings.

HICKORY NUT CAKE.
MRS. F. G. SLACK.

One and a half cups butter, 3 cups sugar, 1 cup milk, 5 cups flour, 2 cups of hickory nut meats, 6 eggs, beaten separately, 3 teaspoons of baking powder.

HARRIET'S CAKE.
MRS. H. B. S.

One and a half cup of butter, 3 cups sugar, 1 cup milk, 5 cups flour, 6 eggs, whites and yolks beaten separately, 1 teaspoonful soda, 2 teaspoonsful cream-tartar.

ICING FOR CAKE.

To the white of 1 egg, allow 5 tablespoonfuls of powdered sugar. Put the sugar into the egg before beating it. Stir briskly in a deep bowl. Flavor to taste.

BOILED ICING.
MRS. W. W. MILLS.

Boil 1 cup of sugar in water enough to cover it. Boil until ropy. When boiling pour on the unbeaten white of an egg and beat rapidly to a froth with a knife.

BOILED ICING.
MISS BARBER.

One-half cup of water, 2 cups of sugar. Boil till it strings. Beat in a pan set in cold water till it is cooled. Beat the whites of 2 eggs and stir into the sugar and water.

FROSTING. — Excellent.
MRS. BEMAN GATES.

To the white of 1 egg add 4 tablespoons of powdered sugar, full. Mix sugar and egg without beating the egg. Beat together till the frosting drops from the spoon, and makes little mountains standing alone.

ICING FOR CAKE.
MRS. F. G. SLACK.

One-fourth pound of sugar to white of 1 egg. Beat the white to a froth. Add sugar and beat until stiff. Never fails.

SOFT FROSTING WITHOUT EGGS.
MRS. NORTHROP.

One cup of sugar, ¼ cup of sweet milk. Boil from 5 to 8 minutes. When it "hairs", it is done. (Take a little on the finger and press it.) When it is partially cool add the flavoring. Beat very hard until white. If too thick to spread nicely, add a little milk.

FROSTING FOR ANY CAKE.
MRS. EATON.

When white of 1 egg is beaten, stir in spoonful by spoonful 10 teaspoons of sifted pulverized sugar. Beat thoroughly. Spinkle in ⅛ of a teaspoon of cream of tartar, add ⅓ of a teaspoon of water, drop by drop, stirring all the while.

ICE CREAM CAKE.
MRS. HOLDEN.

One-half cup of butter, 1 cup of sugar, ½ cup of milk, 3 eggs, 1 teaspoonful of cream of tartar, ½ teaspoonful of soda, 2 cups of flour.

LADY CAKE.
MRS. A. G. GARD.

Two cups of flour, 1½ cups of sugar, ½ cup of sweet milk, ½ cup of butter, 3 eggs, 1 large teaspoonful of baking powder. Try it.

NUT JUMBLES.
MRS. F. G. SLACK.

One-half pound of sugar, ½ pound butter, 8 eggs, add ½ pound chopped almonds and a little lemon juice. Stir in lightly from ½ to ¾ of a pound of flour. Flavor with rose water or orange flower water. Cocoanut can take the place of the almonds if preferred.

DAPHNE'S JUMBLES.

One and a half pounds flour, 1 pound sugar, ¾ pound butter, 4 yolks and 2 whites of eggs, nutmeg, 1 glass full of rose water. Roll them thick with powdered sugar, and bake on tins.

LEMON JELLY CAKE.
MISS IRISH.

Two cups sugar, ½ cup butter, 1 cup milk, 3 cups flour, 3 eggs. Makes 5 layers. For the jelly, grate the rind and use the juice of

Cakes and Icings.

two large lemons. 1 cup sugar, 1 egg, 1 teaspoon butter, ½ cup water, 1 tablespoon flour, mixed with a little water, and boil till it thickens.

JUMBLES.
MRS. B. GATES.

One-half pound of butter, ½ pound sugar, 1 pound flour, 4 eggs. Save some of the sugar to sprinkle on after rolling.

JELLY ROLL.
MRS. D. B. TORPY.

One pint granulated sugar, 1 pint flour, ½ teacup cold water, 1 teaspoon baking powder, 6 eggs.

JAM CAKE.
MISS MARY SLACK, KENTUCKY.

One cup of butter, 2 cups brown sugar, 3 eggs, 1 cup sweet cream, 4 cups flour, 1 cup jam, 1 cup raisins, ½ cup citron, 1 tablespoonful of cinnamon, 1 tablespoonful cloves, 1 tablespoonful baking powder. Bake 2 hours.

MOTHER'S LOAF CAKE.
MRS. H. B. SHIPMAN.

Three pounds flour, 2 pounds sugar, 1¾ pounds butter, 1½ pounds raisins, 1½ pint yeast, 1½ pint warm milk, 3 eggs, 3 nutmegs. Mix sugar and butter together, and use one-half when you wet up your cake, at night. Put in a warm place to rise. Beat well in the morning, and add the remainder of the sugar and butter, also the eggs. Let it rise the second time. When light, just before baking, put in a half teaspoonful of soda. Bake in loaves.

MRS. GOVERNOR MEIGS'S LOAF CAKE—1830.
DAPHNE.

Make up 4 pounds of dough the night before. Next morning put the dough in a wooden bread bowl and mix with it 1½ pounds of butter and 2 pounds of sugar. Then break 7 eggs and put the yolks in, 1 saucer full of every kind of spice, 1 teacup of flour. Then beat up the whites of the 7 eggs and stir the whole up well. 1 pound of raisins, stoned, and well floured. Put this in buttered cake pan and let it stand 3 hours. Then bake it 2 hours. Give it two good coats of icing. Flavor with lemon.

LOAF CAKE BY MEASURE.

MRS. G. DANA.

Two cups milk, 2 cups sugar, ½ cup yeast. Make into a batter at night. In the morning, add 1 cup butter, 1 cup lard, 2 cups sugar, 2 eggs and spices and fruit. This makes 4 loaves.

FRENCH LOAF CAKE.

MRS. ISRAEL WATERS.

Five cups powdered sugar, 3 cups fresh butter, 2 cups sweet milk, 10 cups dried and sifted flour, 6 eggs, 3 nutmegs, 1 teaspoon soda, 1 pound raisins, ¼ pound citron. Stir sugar and butter to a cream add part of the flour with the milk a little warm and the beaten yolks of eggs, then add the rest of the flour, beaten whites of eggs, spice and soda and last of all, the fruit. This makes 4 loaves. Bake 1 hour. More fruit improves it. Use of currants 1 pound.

LIGHT CAKE—13 LOAVES.

MRS. I. W. ANDREWS.

Eight pounds of flour, 5 pounds of sugar, 3 pounds of butter, 1¼ pounds lard, 3 pints of milk, 1 quart of yeast, 8 eggs, 4 nutmegs, 1½ ounces of mace. Mix two pounds of sugar and all the lard in the flour. Add the milk, with the yeast and eggs beaten together. Let it rise, then add your butter and sugar after being well mixed. Add the fruit after second rising. If too rich leave out ½ pound of butter and ¼ pound of lard.

R. E. LEE CAKE.

MISS MARY SLACK, KENTUCKY.

Make batter same as for jelly cake. Squeeze the juice from 4 lemons and 4 oranges. Strain on 1 lb. sugar. Stir until dissolved. Grate 1 cocoanut. Bake cake in jelly cake pans, and as each one is baked, spread on a layer of the juice and sugar, then sprinkle cocoanut over it and drop some of the juice over cocoanut. Then take another layer of cake, and so on until all the cakes are used. Spread icing or sprinkle sugar over the top.

LOAF CAKE.

Three cups bread dough, 2 cups sugar, 1 cup butter, 2 eggs, ½ cup milk, ½ lb. raisins, teaspoon soda. Spice to taste.

Cakes and Icings.

MARBLE CAKE.
MRS. J. L. RECKARD.

WHITE — One cup butter, 2 cups sugar, 4 cups flour, 1 cup sweet milk, whites of 7 eggs, 3 teaspoons baking powder.

DARK — One cup molasses, 1 cup butter, 1 cup sweet milk, 2 cups dark brown sugar, 5 cups flour, 2 tablespoons cinnamon, 2 of allspice, 1 of cloves, 1 of nutmeg, 3 teaspoons baking powder. This will fill a six-quart pan. Put a layer of the white and add the dark and white according to fancy.

OX EYES.
MRS. S. P. HILDRETH.

Two cups of sugar, 2 cups of butter, 3½ cups of flour, 6 eggs, 1 teaspoon soda, nutmeg. Drop on buttered paper and put a raisin in the center of each cake.

ORANGE CAKE.
MRS. HAWKS.

Two coffee cups of sugar, 2 coffee cups of flour, ½ cup of water, grated peel and juice of 1 orange, 5 eggs, 2 teaspoons of baking powder. Stir beaten yolks thoroughly with warmed sugar, add water with the grated rind and juice of the orange mingled, mix in well ½ the flour, then ½ the whites beaten stiff, then very lightly, the rest of the flour, and whites of the eggs.

CREAM. — Dissolve ⅔ of a sheet of isinglass in ⅓ of a teacup of boiling water, strain, add grated peel and juice of 1 orange. Add nough powdered sugar to make it thick as icing. Some use instead, a plain white frosting, flavored with orange juice.

PINE APPLE CAKE.
MRS. F. G. SLACK.

Make by recipe for Angel's Food and bake in layers.

FILLING.—Buy grated pine-apple, press *all* the juice out in hair sieve, add 2 or 3 tablespoons of icing.

POUND CAKE.
MISS IRISH.

One and one-half cups of sugar, 1 cup of butter, ½ cup of milk, 2 cups of flour, 4 eggs, 2 teaspoonfuls of baking powder. Add fruit and citron, if you like.

POUND CAKE.
MRS. WM. R. PUTNAM.

One pound of sugar, 1 pound of flour, $\frac{3}{4}$ of a pound of butter, 8 eggs, nutmeg. Rub butter and sugar together till very light, add yolks of eggs, spice, and part of flour, then the beaten whites, and remainder of flour. Beat well together.

RUSK.
MRS. WM. R. PUTNAM.

One pint of milk, 1 teacup of butter, $2\frac{1}{2}$ cups of sugar, 4 eggs, yeast. Make the milk into a sponge.

ROSE CAKES.
MRS. H. B. S.

One cup of butter, 2 cups of sugar, 5 eggs, leaving out $\frac{1}{2}$ the whites, 1 gill of rose water, a little flour. Roll in sugar.

PERFECTION SPONGE CAKE.
MRS. F. G. SLACK.

Six eggs, 1 pint flour, 1 pint sugar, 2 tablespoonfuls water. Beat the sugar and yolks well together. Beat the whites separately. Then put the whites into the sugar and yolks and beat a good while. Then stir in the flour, only enough to mix well. Bake quick in hot oven. Bake in loaf or in sheets.

SPONGE CAKE ROLL.
HOUSEKEEPER'S FRIEND.

Three eggs, 1 cup sugar, 1 cup flour, 1 teaspoon butter, 1 teaspoon baking powder. Spread in a turkey pan and bake quickly. Roll while hot with currant jelly or jelly for roll. 1 cup sugar, 1 egg, juice of 1 lemon, 1 teaspoon cold water. Stir on the fire until it thickens.

HOT WATER SPONGE CAKE.
MRS. BEACH.

Two eggs, 1 cup of sugar, 1 cup of flour, $\frac{1}{2}$ cup of water nearly boiling, 1 teaspoonful of baking powder, lemon or vanilla. Beat the eggs separately, add sugar, etc., then flour and hot water alternately, a little at a time and bake in a quick oven.

DAPHNE'S SPONGE CAKE.

Six eggs, 1 pint of flour before it is sifted, 1 pint of sugar, ½ teacup water. Heat the flour and sugar, then rub the sugar and the yolks of the eggs together for a very long time, till almost white. Grate in ½ of the nutmeg after you add the water, and juice ½ a lemon. Beat the whites till very stiff, then put in ½ the whites and ½ the flour (very lightly), then stir in (very lightly) the rest of the flour and (partially) stir in the rest of the eggs. This is better baked in a loaf, with icing with a little lemon extract in it.

VELVET SPONGE CAKE.

MRS. DANA.

Two cups of sugar, whites of 3 eggs, yellows of 6 eggs, 1 cup boiling water, 2½ cups of flour, 1 tablespoon of baking powder. Beat the yolks a little, add the sugar and then beat 15 minutes. Add the 3 beaten whites and the cup of water just before the flour. Flavor with extract of lemon. Bake in 3 layers. Make icing of 3 whites of eggs beaten stiff, and 6 dessertspoonfuls pulverized sugar to each egg.

SPONGE MOLASSES CAKE.

A large spoon very full of shortening, 1 cup molasses, 1 large teaspoon soda (heaping full) dissolved in a cup of boiling hot water, 2½ cups of flour.

SPICE CAKE.

MRS. R. B. HART.

Two cups sugar, 3 cups flour, ½ cup butter, 1 cup milk or water, yolks of 5 eggs, 2 teaspoons of cloves, 3 teaspoons of cinnamon, 2 teaspoons of allspice, 3 teaspoons of ginger, 1 nutmeg, 2 teaspoons baking powder. Bake in 3 layers, using icing between.

SPICE CAKE.

MRS. JOHN EATON.

One cup of sugar, ½ cup of molasses, ½ cup of butter, 2 or 3 eggs, ½ cup of milk, sweet or sour, 1½ teaspoon soda, 1½ teaspoon cinnamon, 1½ teaspoon nutmeg, 1 teaspoon of salt, 1 teaspoon of cloves, 1 cup of raisins. Have the batter a little stiff. About 2 cups of flour.

SPICE CAKE.

MRS. H. B. SHIPMAN.

One cup butter, 3 cups sugar, 5 cups flour, 1 of sweet milk, 5 eggs,

1 pound of raisins, chopped fine, 3 teaspoonfuls baking powder, 1 tablespoonful cinnamon, 1 teaspoonful cloves, 1 teaspoonful nutmeg.

SPICE CAKE.
MRS. H. C. VINCENT.

Two cups brown sugar, 2 cups flour, 1 cup sour milk, ½ cup butter, 1 teaspoonful soda, yolks of 6 eggs, 1 teaspoonful of all kinds of spices or as much as you like. Bake in layers, with frosting between.

SEED CAKE.
MRS. B. GATES.

Four eggs, 4 cups of sugar, 1 cup of butter, ½ cup of milk, 4 spoonfuls of caraway seed, baking powder, flour enough to roll well. Roll thin.

SEED CAKES.
MRS. H. B. SHIPMAN.

Three and a half pounds flour, 1¼ pound sugar, ½ pint water, 1 teaspoon of soda, plenty of caraway seed.

SAND TARTS.
MRS. HARRY THOMAS.

One pound of butter rubbed into 2 pounds of flour, add 2 pounds of sugar, and wet the whole with whites of 3 eggs and the yolks of 4. Roll very thin, cut in diamond shapes, glaze with the white of 1 egg, cover with nuts chopped fine and ground cinnamon.

SAND TARTS.
MRS. W. G. WAY.

Two cups of light brown sugar, 1 cup of butter, 3 eggs, leaving out 1 of the whites to spread on top, 3 cups of flour, a little baking powder. Work the butter, sugar, yolks of eggs, and 1 white, flour and baking powder all together. Roll out thin, spread on the white of egg beaten to a stiff froth. Sprinkle over this ground cinnamon and granulated sugar. Cut in squares with a knife and bake in a moderate oven.

SUNSHINE CAKE.
MISS M. ROSS, CINCINNATI.

Take a handful of industry, mix it thoroughly with family love, season well with good nature and mutual forbearance. Gradually stir

Cakes and Icings.

in smiles, jokes, and laughter, to make it light; take care these ingredients do not run over, or it will make a cloud instead of what you wish. Follow this recipe carefully, and you will have an excellent supply of sunshine, warranted to keep in all weather.

MRS. DE STEIGUER'S CAKE.

One cup of butter, 2 cups of sugar, 5 eggs, stirred in separately, 1 cup of corn starch, flour to make it right consistency, flavoring to taste.

TEA CAKE.
MRS. GEO. HARRISON.

One cup of sugar, 1 tablespoon of butter, 2 cups of flour, 3 eggs beaten separately, ½ cup of milk, 2 teaspoons of baking powder.

TEA CAKES.
MRS. H. WHEELER, KY.

Three eggs separated, 1 teacup of sugar, 1 teacup of butter, 1 quart of flour, 1 teaspoon of soda, 1 teaspoon of baking powder, vanilla. Roll thin. Cover with icing and scatter colored caraway seeds over them for children's parties.

TEA CAKE.
MRS. H. FEARING.

Four cups of flour, 1 cup of butter, 1 cup of sour milk, 2½ cups of sugar, 3 eggs, 1 teaspoon of soda.

MRS. VINTON'S CAKE. 1835.

One pound of flour, ¾ pound sugar, ½ pound of butter, 6 eggs, 1 cup sour cream, 1 nutmeg, 1 teaspoonful soda, 2 teaspoonfuls cream tartar. To be baked quick in tin shapes. Raisins if you choose.

MOTHER'S BEST WHITE CAKE.
MRS. A. T. NYE.

One pound of flour, 1 pound of sugar, ¾ pound of butter, 15 eggs, whites only.

WHITE PERFECTION CAKE.
RECOMMENDED BY MRS. NORTHROP, BELPRE, AND MRS. A. W. KING.

Three cups of sugar, 1 cup of butter (coffee cup), 1 cup of milk (sweet), 1 cup of corn-starch, 3 cups of flour, 1 teaspoon soda (small spoon), 2 teaspoons cream tartar, whites of 12 eggs. Flavor with extract of lemon or almond. Cream the butter and sugar. Add the corn-starch which has been previously moistened with half the milk. Dissolve the soda in the other half of the milk, then add to the mixture, then add the flour and cream of tartar, sifted together, and lastly the eggs beaten to a stiff froth.

WHITE CAKE.

MRS. H. B. SHIPMAN.

One cup butter, 3 cups sugar, 5 of flour, 1½ cup milk and the whites of 6 eggs beaten very stiff. 1 teaspoonful soda, 2 teaspoonfuls cream tartar.

WHITE MOUNTAIN CAKE.

MRS. A. W. KING.

One cup butter (coffee cup), 3 cups sugar, 1 cup sweet milk, 4½ cups flour, 4½ teaspoons baking powder, whites of 10 eggs. Cream the butter and sugar, add half the milk, sift the flour and baking powder together, add part of it, then the milk, then the remainder of the flour. Lastly the eggs. Bake in layers. This may be varied by taking ½ the mixture and adding raisins, currants and spices to taste. Put together the layers with frosting. Sift your flour and sugar 2 or 3 times before measuring.

WHITE NUT CAKE.

MRS. ROSSETER.

Whites of 6 eggs, 2 cups sugar, 1 cup butter, 1 cup milk, 3 cups flour, 2 teaspoonfuls baking powder. Flavor with almond. 1½ pound English walnuts broken, not too fine.

WASHINGTON CAKE.

MRS. H. CHAPIN.

One pound sugar, 1 pound flour, ¾ pound butter, 6 eggs, 1 pint rich milk, 1 teaspoon soda, cinnamon and nutmeg.

Puddings and Pudding Sauces.

"THE PROOF OF THE PUDDING LIES IN THE EATING."

"*Every leading dish has its kindred and antagonistic one.*"

AN ATTRACTIVE PUDDING.

MRS. D. B. WOODBRIDGE, DETROIT.

Use *pink* gelatine. Make a boiled custard, with the yolks of 4 eggs, 1 pint of milk and sugar to taste. Soak $\frac{1}{3}$ of a box of gelatine in a little cold water, then pour over $\frac{3}{4}$ of a cup of boiling water. When the custard is cold, add to it the gelatine and the whites of 4 eggs, beaten stiff. Flavor with vanilla. Stir together and pour into a mould. It will settle into 3 layers making an attractive pudding.

BAKED CUSTARD.

MISS MARTHA PUTNAM.

Five eggs well beaten and run through a gravy strainer, $\frac{3}{4}$ cup of sugar, cinnamon, nutmeg, salt. Put the above into a two quart bowl and fill with sweet milk. Fill cups from this and set in a pan of hot water and bake one hour.

BIRD'S NEST PUDDING.

MRS. FRAZYER.

One quart milk, 4 eggs, $\frac{1}{2}$ nutmeg, $\frac{1}{2}$ teaspoon salt, 2 tablespoons butter, 3 tablespoons sugar. Place these, with the exception of the eggs, on the fire until it reaches boiling point, then stir in quickly the eggs, well beaten, and stand away to cool. Then cover a dish with pie paste and place in apples enough to cover the bottom of the dish, the cavity of each filled with a small piece of the paste, in which place four or five dried currants. Pour over the whole the custard and bake one hour and a half.

MORGANZA BAKED CUSTARD — 1812.

MRS. DUDLEY WOODBRIDGE.

Nine eggs minus 4 whites, beaten up, whites and yellows together, with about 12 heaping teaspoonfuls of sugar. Take 1 quart of new milk, let it come to a boil. Then pour the milk into the eggs, stirring them briskly while doing so.. Put your custard in cups, and grate a little nutmeg over the top, set them into a pan partly filled with hot water. Bake them in a moderate oven.

BOSTON SAGO PUDDING.

MRS. JOHN MEANS, ASHLAND.

One large teacup of sago, 4 pints of boiling water poured on it. Set it over a kettle of boiling water and cook it till it is soft and clear. Then stir in 2 teacups of sugar and 1 teaspoon of essence of lemon. Peel 12 apples and pour over them the sago. Then bake till the apples are done. Eat with cream—hot or cold.

BROWN BETTY.

MRS. GEO. DANA.

Pare the apples and chop them fine. Then put in a well greased pan, a layer of apples, an inch thick. Sprinkle over it sugar and spice. Then add a layer of fine bread crumbs and then another layer of apples, sugar and spice, etc., etc. Put on the top a piece of butter, the size of an egg, and pour over the whole a teacup of water. Bake two hours and eat with sauce.

SAUCE.

Take twice as much sugar as butter, then beat up 1 egg, very light, with any spice preferred. Add a very little boiling water, and hold the sauce over hot water, which is boiling, beating it very hard for a few minutes till it is hot.

BAKED APPLES.

MRS. H. C. EVANS.

One tablespoonful flour stirred into 1 teaspoonful melted butter, 1 teaspoonful ground cinnamon, 4 large tablespoonfuls sugar, ½ pint boiling water. Stir all together and let simmer a few minutes. Pour over baked apples while hot, before serving.

BATTER PUDDING.

MRS. CAROLINE DAWES.

Two cups sour cream, 1 teaspoon salt, 2 teaspoons soda, 3 eggs. Flour enough to make rather a stiff batter. Bake. Eaten with sauce.

STEAMED BERRY PUDDING.

MRS. DE STEIGUER.

Four cups flour, 1 cup sugar, 1 cup milk, 2 eggs, 2 tablespoons melted butter, 4 teaspoons baking powder, 1 teaspoon salt. Stir fruit to suit the taste into the batter, pour it into a buttered pan, and steam 1½ hours.

SAUCE FOR SAME. — One cup sugar, ½ cup butter, 2 tablespoons corn starch, wet with cold water. Add boiling water, place it over the fire till it boils. Flavor to taste.

BLACKBERRY PUDDING.

MRS. M. M. POND.

A nice blackberry pudding is made of ½ cup of sour cream (good), 1 even teaspoonful of soda, same of salt, 1 heaping tablespoonful of sugar, and flour enough to make a stiff batter; lastly, stir in 1 pint of nice large berries—slightly. Put in a pudding dish and steam ¾ of an hour. Serve with sugar and cream.

BAKED APPLE DUMPLING.

MRS. EDGERTON.

Core as many small apples as will fit into a pudding dish. Make pie crust and incase each apple in a piece of the crust, having first put a little butter, some sugar and ground cinnamon in each apple. Mix water, butter, sugar and spice as for sauce and pour some of it over the dumplings. Bake till done, putting more of the sauce over them as it cooks away. Serve hot.

BOILED CUSTARD.

Five eggs to a quart of milk, 5 tablespoons of sugar, add flour when cool. When the custard is done and hot, add a little of the beaten egg, then heap the rest in spoonfuls, making an uneven surface.

BREAD AND BUTTER PUDDING.

A layer of sliced apples, a little nutmeg and sugar, a layer of bread and butter, then a layer of apples, so continue until you have filled your pan, the last layer being apples, add a cup of hot water, sufficient to wet the bread. Bake 1 hour in a moderate oven.

A delicious pudding is made by using rhubarb instead of apples. Cut up the rhubarb *without taking off the skin*. Slice as you would for pies.

A NICE CHEAP PUDDING.

MRS. F. G. SLACK.

Three tablespoonfuls melted butter, 1 cup of sugar mixed with butter, 1 egg well beaten, 1 pint flour, 1 cup of sweet milk, 1 teaspoonful of soda, 2 teaspoonfuls of cream of tartar. Beat well, and bake 30 minutes. To be eaten hot with sauce.

CHOCOLATE PUDDING.

MRS. H. W. ROSSETER.

Two cups of bread crumbs, 1 cup of sugar, 1 quart of milk, 5 eggs, 3 tablespoonfuls of grated chocolate. Boil bread and milk until it thickens. After it is cool stir in the beaten yolks of 5 and whites of 2 eggs with the sugar, add the chocolate. Bake ½ hour. Beat 3 whites, 5 tablespoonfuls of sugar, and 1 teaspoonful of vanilla. Spread over the top and brown. Eat cold with cream.

CORN STARCH PUDDING.

MRS. D. E. BEACH.

One pint of milk, 2 tablespoons of corn starch, ½ cup of sugar. Flavor. Boil the milk, adding the sugar and corn starch, and when thick, stir in lightly ½ of a grated cocoanut and the beaten whites of 3 or 4 eggs. Mould, and eat cold with cream.

CRAWFORDSVILLE SNOW PUDDING.

One cup of Cooper's gelatine, after it is broken into fine bits. Pour 3½ cups of water over it and let it stand till dissolved. Add 2 cups of sugar, and juice of 2 lemons. Strain and set in a cool place till it begins to jelly, then add the well beaten whites of 3 eggs. Stir in well, and turn into a mould.

COTTAGE PUDDING.

One cup of sugar, 1 tablespoonful of butter, 1 cup of sweet milk, 1 pint of flour, 2 eggs, 2 heaping teaspoonfuls of baking powder. Serve with rich sauce.

CUP CUSTARD.

MRS. BARBER.

One quart of milk, 4 eggs, 1 cup of sugar, 1 salt spoon of salt. Boil the milk. Beat the eggs with the sugar and salt till very light and add the hot milk slowly. Pour into small cups which have been set in a dripping pan, making 8 teacupsful. Grate nutmeg over the top of each. Pour boiling water into the pan after it has been set into the oven. Bake slowly, testing (after the first 20 minutes) with a knife blade. The moment the knife blade comes out smooth, they are done. The more slowly they are cooked the more creamy they are.

ORANGE CUSTARD.

MISS BARBER.

Divide and subdivide sweet oranges. Place them in a deep dish and pour a rich corn starch custard over them. Bake slowly.

BOILED CUSTARD.

MRS. EDGERTON.

One quart new milk, yolks of five eggs, whites of seven eggs (two of these whites are for the meringue), 6 tablespoons of sugar, vanilla flavoring, 1 teaspoonful to a pint, heat the milk almost to boiling. Beat the yolks well, stir in the sugar and stir carefully into the milk, removing it from the fire to do so. Stir in the whites of five eggs, after beating them to a froth. Return the whole to the fire, stir carefully until it is thick, but not until it breaks; pour in the vanilla now. Pour into glass cups. Whip the whites of the two eggs remaining to a meringue with a heaping tablespoonful of powdered sugar, and when the custard is cold, pile a little of this on the top of each cup. A preserved strawberry or cherry or a little bright colored jelly can be placed on the top of each.

CUSTARD.

One quart of milk, 4 eggs, beaten separately. Beat with the yolks ½ cup sugar. Stirr into the egg scalded milk, spoonful by spoonful, return to sauce pan and cook till thickened. Pour over the oranges. Spread over top the whites, beaten, with enough sugar for a stiff meringue. Place in oven to brown. To be served when cold.

CUSTARD PUDDING.

MRS. BENJAMIN DANA.

One quart of milk, 1 pint of flour, 6 eggs, and a little salt. To be eaten with rich sauce.

CORN STARCH PUDDING.

MRS. CUTLER.

One quart of milk; take one-half the milk and heat it, when nearly boiling add 2 tablespoonfuls of corn starch, dissolved in cold milk and a little sugar. When ready to take off, stir in the whites of 2 eggs, beaten stiff. Make a custard of the other one-half quart of milk and the yolks of the eggs, and pour over the pudding, when cold.

This same pudding is delicious with whipped cream poured over it. Take ½ a bowl full of cream, beat it with a Dover egg beater, and as the cream grows light and puffy take it off and sweeten it, and flavor it with vanilla.

DELMONICO PUDDING.

One quart scalded milk, 3 tablespoons corn starch, moistened with a little cold milk; stir into the boiling milk the beaten yolks of 5 eggs, 4 tablespoons of sugar; stir it all well together, then take it off and flavor it; pour into a pudding dish; place over the top of this the whites of 5 eggs, the juice of the lemons and a heaping tablespoon of sugar, beaten to a stiff froth; set this into your oven and brown it. It may take from 5 to 12 minutes to do it.

EVE'S PUDDING.

MRS. H. L. HART.

Six eggs, 6 apples, 6 ounces of bread crumbs, 6 ounces of currants, 6 ounces of sugar, salt and nutmeg. Boil 3 hours. Serve with sauce.

FRUIT PUDDING.

MISS IRISH.

One cup of sweet milk, 1 cup of sugar, 2 cups of flour, 2 eggs well beaten, 2 tablespoonfuls of baking powder. Put any kind of small fruit—tart apples are perhaps the nicest—in a well buttered dish, pour the batter over it and steam 1 hour. Serve with sauce. One-half the receipt will do for a family of four or five.

FRUIT PUDDING.

MRS. M. P. WELLS.

One cup of molasses, 1 cup of sweet milk, ½ cup of butter, 2 cups of raisins, seeded, 4 cups of flour, 1 teaspoonful of soda, 2 teaspoonfuls of cream of tartar, a little salt, cinnamon, cloves and nutmeg. Steam 4 or 5 hours. Serve with rich sauce.

FIG PUDDING.

MRS. F. G. SLACK.

One teacup of suet, 1 teacup of molasses, 2 eggs, 1 teaspoon of soda, 1 teacup of milk, 3 teacups of flour, 1 teacup of figs cut the size of raisins. Steam 2 or 3 hours.

FLOATING ISLAND.

MRS. EDGERTON.

Whites of 9 eggs, 9 teaspoons of jelly, 4½ teaspoons of sugar, 1 teaspoon of essence of lemon. Beat this 1 hour, and have a glass dish of rich cream and place the float upon it.

FLOATING ISLAND.

One quart of milk, as soon as it boils stir in the yolks of four beaten eggs, ¾ of cup of sugar, 1 teaspoon of salt, let them boil up a moment, stir constantly, pour into a covered dish, season with vanilla. Have your whites well beaten and drop on the top of the custard by the spoonful, then cover immediately. The steam thus confined will cook the islands sufficiently.

FRUIT PUDDING.

MRS. LAURA TORRANCE, MONTREAL.

One-half pound of figs minced, rather less than ½ pound of suet, ¼ pound of brown sugar, ½ pound of bread crumbs, 1 cup of milk, 1 ounce of orange peel, 5 eggs, and a little ground cinnamon and ginger. Mince the figs small. Boil 5 hours. Serve with sauce. Six ounces of suet is sufficient. It is very good without the orange peel.

FOUR MINUTE PUDDING.

Three tablespoonfuls of corn starch, 1 quart of milk, dissolve the corn starch in some of the milk and mix with it a little salt and 3 eggs well beaten. Heat the remainder of the milk in a bucket set in hot water, add the above preparation and boil 4 minutes, or until it thickens, stirring it briskly. To be eaten with liquid sauce.

GOLD AND SILVER PUDDING.
MRS. H. B. SHIPMAN.

One quart of milk, 6 tablespoonfuls of flour, add a little salt. Take ½ of the milk and let it come to a boiling heat, then add the remainder of the milk and flour stirred together. When this is cool put in the beaten yolks of 6 eggs. Bake about half an hour. For the icing take the whites of 6 eggs, ½ cup of sugar beaten till very stiff. Flavor with lemon. To be eaten cold.

GRAHAM FLOUR PUDDING.
MRS. JOHN EATON.

One and a half cups Graham flour, ½ cup of molasses, ½ cup of butter, ½ cup of sweet milk, 1 egg, 1 teaspoon of soda, 1 cup of raisins, 1 teaspoon of cinnamon, ½ teaspoon of cloves. Steam 2 hours.

GELATINE CUSTARD.
MRS. TURNER.

One cup sugar, 1 pint tepid water, the whites of 4 eggs, ½ package of gelatine dissolved in the water. Beat the whites to a stiff froth and put in the dissolved gelatine and beat all together half an hour. Flavor with lemon or vanilla. Make the yolks into a custard and pour over it.

GRAHAM PUDDING.
MRS. WOODRUFF.

One cup Graham flour, 1 egg, ¾ cup molasses, 1 teaspoon soda, 1 cup sweet milk, salt, 1 cup raisins. Steam 3½ hours. Served with sauce.

HUNTER'S PUDDING.
MRS. GALLAHER, BELLAIRE.

One cup of butter, 1 egg, 1 cup of molasses, 1 cup of raisins, 1 cup of sour milk, 2 teaspoons soda, all kinds of spice. Make a stiff batter and steam 3 hours. Serve with sauce.

HENRIETTA ROBBINS'S PUDDING.

Mix 5 spoons of flour and 5 spoons of milk with 5 well beaten eggs, mix the yolks with the flour and milk, then turn 1 quart boiling milk

Puddings and Pudding Sauces.

upon it, after which stir in the well beaten whites with it. Bake 15 minutes. To be used immediately with sauce.

INDIAN TAPIOCA PUDDING.

MRS. ROSSETER.

Boil 1 pint of milk into which stir 5 large spoonsful corn meal which has been wet up with ½ pint cold milk, add ½ cup tapioca (soaked) and ⅔ cup of molasses, salt, then add ½ pint more of cold milk. Bake and eat while hot with plenty of butter.

From the American Frugal Housewife.—By Mrs. Child, Boston, Mass. 1836.

BAKED INDIAN PUDDING.

FURNISHED BY MRS. D. H. GARD, COLUMBUS, O.

Scald a quart of milk, (skimmed milk will do) and stir in 7 tablespoons of sifted Indian meal, 1 teaspoon of salt, 1 teacup of molasses, 1 great spoon of ginger or sifted cinnamon. Bake 3 or 4 hours. If you want whey you must be sure and pour in a little cold milk after it is all mixed. A little chopped apple can be added which makes it very nice.

BAKED INDIAN PUDDING.

MRS. I. H. NYE.

Two quarts milk, 7 tablespoons corn meal. Stir in the milk while boiling, when cool add 1 tablespoon flour, 4 eggs, nutmeg or other spices, 1 teacup molasses, butter size of an egg. Bake 2 hours.

KING GEORGE'S PUDDING.

MRS. CUTLER.

One pint of bread crumbs, ½ pint of flour, 1 teaspoon baking powder sifted in the flour, a little salt, ½ pound raisins, ¼ pound currants, ¼ pound chopped suet, 1 coffee cup of milk, 1 egg. Tie tightly in a bag and boil 3 hours, or in a covered tin mould, in water, one hour and a half.

PUDDING SAUCE.

MISS IRISH.

One cup butter, 2 cups sugar beaten to a cream, add 2 eggs beaten very light. Stir in 4 tablespoons boiling water and flavor to taste. Instead of water one may use syrup left over from canned fruits.

PUDDING SAUCE.

MRS. H. L. HART.

Two dessertspoons flour, 3 dessertspoons sugar, a small piece of butter, a little salt. Mix sugar, flour and butter with 2 spoons cold water and add 1 pint boiling water. Flavor to taste.

PUDDING SAUCE.

OLD SOUTH CH. COOK BOOK.

One tablespoon of butter, ½ pint sugar, grated peel and juice of one lemon, ½ pint water, boil, cool a little and stir in yolk and white of a well beaten egg.

PUDDING SAUCE.

To 1 teacup brown sugar, 1 dessertspoon flour, rubbed smoothly together. Over this pour a little boiling water, stirring. When boiled add a large lump of butter, teaspoon of vinegar and nutmeg.

PUDDING SAUCE.

One cup sugar, ½ cup butter, 2 eggs, ½ lemon. Rub butter and sugar to a cream, add eggs and beat very light. Put the same in a cup over the boiling tea kettle and stir often. Just before serving add grated rind and juice of lemon.

For apple dumplings use more sugar.

LEMON SAUCE.

MRS. T. H. HAWKS.

One large cup of sugar, nearly half a cup of butter, 1 egg, 1 lemon, all the juice and half the grated peel, 3 tablespoonfuls boiling water, cream the butter and sugar and beat in the egg, beaten very light, add the lemon; beat hard ten minutes and add one spoonful of the water at a time. Put in tin pail and set within the uncovered top of the tea kettle, which you must keep boiling until the steam heats the sauce very hot—but not to boil. Stir constantly.

ANOTHER LEMON SAUCE.

MRS. T. H. HAWKS.

Take 1 cup of sugar and ½ cup butter, and when it is creamed stir it into boiling lemonade, made of 1 lemon and ½ pint of water.

PUDDING SAUCES.

MRS. W. W. MILLS.

FOAM SAUCE.—One teacup of sugar, ⅔ teacup of butter, 1 teaspoon flour. Beat together till smooth, then place on the fire and stir in rapidly 3 gills of boiling water. Season with nutmeg, or to suit the taste.

ANOTHER.—The beaten whites of 2 eggs, 1 cup of sugar, 1 cup of cream, beaten to a stiff froth. Flavor to taste.

SAUCE FOR STEAMED DUMPLINGS.

One-half cup of butter, beaten to a cream, ½ cup of pulverized sugar, 1 spoonful of hot water; beat well. Add grated nutmeg on top.

MRS. HORACE NORTON'S PUDDING.

Juice of 3 lemons, ¾ of a pound of sugar, whites of 8 eggs. Beat to a light froth and bake 10 minutes. This is complete, or you can make of the yolks a soft custard and pour over when served.

ORANGE PUDDING.

Take six large juicy oranges, slice them, removing seeds and rind. Place them in a pudding dish with plenty of sugar between layers.

ORANGE CORN STARCH PUDDING.

Slice oranges over the bottom of the pudding dish, and sweeten sufficiently. Pour over it the above mixture, using only the yolks of the eggs, and a cup of sugar. Make a meringue of the whites of the eggs. Pour over the pudding and brown slightly. To be eaten cold.

PORTLAND PUDDING.

One cup of chopped suet, 1 cup of raisins (chopped), 1 cup of milk, 1 cup of molasses, 4 cups of flour, ½ teaspoon of soda. Mix well together. Add the soda last and boil the pudding 3 hours.

POOR MAN'S PUDDING.

Chop and fill a small baking pan with apples. Make a batter with 1 egg and 1 pint of milk, and 3 cups of flour, and pour over the apples, and bake it.

POOR MAN'S PUDDING.

MRS. BEACH.

One cup of molasses, 1 cup of suet or butter, 1 cup of milk, 1 cup of raisins, 4 cups of flour, some spice, 1 teaspoon of soda dissolved in the molasses. Boil 4 hours. Eat with sauce.

PRUNE PUDDING.

E. W. C.

Stew ½ pound of prunes till they are very soft. Put them through a colander, sweeten and flavor with vanilla. Beat the whites of 4 eggs very stiff, then beat in the prunes, place in a dish and bake till it will not stick to a straw. Make a custard of the yolks and after the prunes are baked pour it over them. If rightly made this will be a light frothy dish with custard dressing.

PEACH PUDDING.

MRS. H. C. EVANS.

One pint of milk boiled, 2 tablespoonfuls of corn starch, a little butter, 1 cup of sugar, 3 eggs. Stir into the boiling milk. Fill the pudding dish with peaches halved. Cover with sugar. Pour over them the batter. Crack pits and put meats on top.

RICE PUDDING.

MRS. E. S. McINTOSH.

One and a half cups of rice. Put on the stove in cold water and let simmer 1 hour. Then add 3 pints of *new* milk and let boil for ½ hour. Put into a large pan 4 eggs, 2 teaspoonfuls of salt, ½ of a nutmeg, 5 large tablespoonfuls of sugar, 1 pint of raisins that have been already put on the stove in cold water and come to a scald, add rich milk, part cream if you have it) enough to fill your pan. Bake 1½ hours. Stir twice while baking, to keep the raisins from settling to the bottom. The above quantity will fill a six quart pan. Half the quantity will be enough for a small family.

RICE PUDDING.

MRS. H. FEARING.

One quart milk, ½ teacup of rice, ½ teacup of sugar, 1 teaspoon of salt. Flavor with nutmeg or vanilla. Bake in a moderate oven from 2 to 3 hours. Stir occasionally. Use a morsel of butter.

Puddings and Pudding Sauces.

RICE PUDDING.
MRS. FANNY NYE POTTER, ZANESVILLE.

One small cup of rice, 1 quart milk, 6 tablespoons sugar, 3 eggs, a pinch of salt, 1 lemon, butter size of an egg. Boil the rice in the milk till soft. The grating of the lemon, yolks of the eggs, and half the sugar, mixed with the rice while hot. The whites with juice of lemon and remainder of sugar.

SUET PUDDING.

One cup chopped suet, 1 cup molasses, 1 cup hot water or milk, 3½ cups flour, 1 cup raisins, 1 teaspoon soda, 2 teaspoons cinnamon, ½ teaspoon cloves. Steam 3 hours.

SUET PUDDING.
MISS IRISH.

One cup molasses, 1 cup suet, 1 cup milk, 3 cups flour, 2 cups raisins or chopped figs, 1 tablespoon soda, 1 tablespoon allspice, 1 tablespoon cinnamon, 1 teaspoonful cloves. Steam 2 hours and serve with a sauce.

SNOW PUDDING.
MRS. H C. EVANS.

One-half box gelatine dissolved in 1 pint of water. Let about ⅓ of the pint of water be put on the gelatine cold, when soft, put the rest of the pint on boiling hot, 1 cup of sugar, juice of 2 lemons. Mix all together and strain. When cold and it begins to stiffen beat it to a froth, then add the whites of 4 eggs beaten to a stiff froth. Beat well together. Put in cups or a mould to cool. Take the yolks of eggs and 1½ pints milk, make custard and pour round it just before serving.

SNOW PUDDING.
MRS. OGBORN.

One box gelatine soaked in a quart of water 1 hour, 2 cups of sugar, pour over 1 pint of boiling water, set it away to cool, when it begins to congeal add the whites of 6 eggs well beaten. Beat until thoroughly mixed.

SAGO PUDDING.

One teacup of sago, 1 quart of cold water, stand 4 hours, then put the same pan on the stove and let it come to boiling point, have a pudding dish with apples sliced, pour the sago over these, you need to salt and sweeten the sago first, put a few bread crumbs over the top. Bake until the apples are tender. Serve with cream.

TAPIOCA PUDDING.

MRS. H. B. SHIPMAN.

One cup tapioca in a pint of milk, set it near the fire to soak, stirring it often. Let it stand 2 or 3 hours, then add a pint of cold milk, 5 eggs, 2 cups sugar, 1 cup raisins, a little salt and spice to your taste. Bake one hour and a half.

TROPICAL SNOW.

MRS. D. E. BEACH.

Eight oranges, 5 bananas, 1 cocoanut, 1 cup of sugar. Slice the bananas thin. Cut the oranges into small pieces. Grate the cocoanut. Arrange the orange, banana and cocoanut in layers, sprinkled with sugar. Have the top layer of cocoanut, with a few slices of banana for ornament.

MRS. H. A. TOWNE'S PUDDING.

Boil ¾ of a cup of butter in 2 tablespoons of flour, stirring all the time, add a tumbler of sweet milk and stir until the consistency of starch. Take from the fire and add the unbeaten yolks of four eggs. Make this in the morning. Before dinner add the whites well beaten and 2 tablespoons of sugar. Bake 25 minutes. Eat with liquid sauce.

TAPIOCA PUDDING.

Take 3 tablespoonfuls of tapioca, soak in ½ cup of water. Take the yolks of 3 eggs and mix with 1 cup of sugar, and a little salt. Stir all together. Add 1 quart of boiling milk, 1 teaspoonful of vanilla. Let it thicken a little, only a few minutes. Beat the whites of the eggs to a stiff froth, add 1 tablespoonful of sugar. Turn the pudding into a dish, drop the frosting on it in spoonsful and set it in the oven to brown slightly. To be eaten cold.

ANOTHER TAPIOCA PUDDING.

One teacup of tapioca soaked in 1 quart of water, 12 apples peeled and cored, a little sugar and cinnamon in each. Bake till about half done. Let the tapioca come to a scald, pour over the apples and bake an hour. To be eaten warm with sauce.

TAPIOCA APPLE PUDDING.

ELIZABETH ANDERSON.

Soak for 2 hours a teacup of tapioca in more than enough water to cover, keeping it warm, (when done the pudding should be trans-

Puddings and Pudding Sauces.

parent; otherwise not sufficient water has been used.) Put in a buttered baking dish alternate layers of the tapioca flavored with vanilla and sliced apples, adding to the batter sugar and small bits of butter. Bake an hour or more—until the apple is done. Serve with cream or sweet sauce.

TAYLOR PUDDING.

One cup of sour milk, 1 cup of suet, 1 cup of molasses, 1 cup of raisins, 2 eggs, 1 teaspoonful of soda, flour enough to make a stiff batter. Steam 3 hours. To be eaten with sauce.

THANKSGIVING PUDDING.

MRS. WEBSTER, MAINE.

Two pounds of raisins after being stoned and cut, 1 pound of beef suet chopped fine, 1 pound of crackers, 8 eggs, 2 nutmegs, ¼ pound of sugar, 1 tablespoon of cinnamon, 1 pint milk, 1 teaspoonful of cloves, salt. Beat eggs very light, then put in ½ the milk and beat both together. Stir in gradually the cracker, then the other ingredients, lastly the remainder of the milk. If not thick enough add a little more cracker. Steam 6 hours.

SAUCE FOR THE ABOVE.

MRS. WEBSTER.

One and one-half pounds of sugar, ¼ cup of butter, yolk of 1 egg. Rub well together and add the white of the egg beaten to a stiff froth. Add 1 cup of boiling water and flavor to taste.

YORKSHIRE PUDDING.

(TO BE EATEN WITH ROAST BEEF.)

MRS. D. H. GARD, COLUMBUS.

Six tablespoons of flour, 4 eggs, and milk enough to make a thin batter. Put 2 tablespoons of lard in a small dripping pan; when the pan is hot pour in the batter. Bake 20 minutes.

CHILI SAUCE.

MRS. DR. SAM'L. HART.

Chop fine 3 dozen ripe tomatos, 2 onions, 3 red peppers. After boiling until a fine pulp, add 2 cups of sugar, 4 teaspoons of salt, 3 cups of vinegar, 2 tablespoons of mace, 2 tablespoons of cinnamon, 2 tablespoons of cloves, 2 ounces of mustard seed, whole. Boil fifteen minutes and seal up.

Preserves and Jellies.

"Will't please your honor, taste of these conserves."
—*Shakespeare.*

Preserves, as our grandmothers used them are obsolete. A general rule for making them was a pound of sugar to a pound of fruit. The fruit peeled and laid in the sugar over night. Simmer over a slow fire taking the fruit out often, cooling on a platter and returning. When the fruit is considered done, remove and boil the syrup down and pour over fruit. When cold put in glass jars. Quinces should be parboiled before adding sugar.

APPLE JELLY.
MRS. A. M. L. BARBER.

Cut a peck of Pippin apples, into quarters after paring and coring them. Put them into enough water to prevent burning, but not enough to make the juice thin; about one quart of water would suffice. When the apples are cooked thoroughly strain through a flannel bag without squeezing. Then to each pint of juice allow ¾ of a pound of sugar. Put the juice on and boil 10 minutes; add the sugar and boil 20 minutes longer; add the juice and peel of 2 fresh lemons, if you choose. A little bunch of rose geranium leaves boiled into it, 2 or 3 minutes before it is done, is nice.

CRANBERRY SAUCE.
MRS. JAMES HOLDEN.

One quart of cranberries, 1½ cups of water; boil fast till broken; then add 1 pint of sugar, and boil up 2 or 3 times.

CRAB APPLE PRESERVES.
MRS. ROSSETER.

Take large crab apples—prick them. To every pound of fruit allow a pound and a half of sugar and one pint of water; boil and skin till clear; then to each pound of fruit the juice and chipped rind of one lemon. Put in the crab apples and boil slowly till tender. Fill your jars half full of fruit and cover with the juice.

CURRANT JELLY.

MRS. BLENNERHASSETT'S.

Place the currants in a stone jar set in hot water; leave it several hours till the skin of the fruit look empty of juice. Put the currants in a flannel jelly bag and let them drip all night, without squeezing. Next morning add 1 pound of sugar to every pint of juice, and boil from 5 to 15 minutes.

Mrs. Blennerhassett's thought the art of making jelly consisted in using the currants before they were thoroughly ripened.

TO PRESERVE CURRANTS.

To 7 pounds of ripe currants add 7 pounds of sugar, 2 pounds of raisins. Put all in a kettle together and let them boil slowly until the fruit is done. Then dip out and cook the syrup 2 or 3 hours.

FOX GRAPE JELLY FOR CAKE.

MRS. ROLSTON.

Pick off of stems and wash. Put in a kettle and add as little water as will do to start them cooking without burning. When soft rub through a sieve. To every pint of the juice add 1 pint of sugar. Return to the kettle and let boil 20 minutes, or until it will harden into jelly.

ORANGE MARMALAD.—(GOOD).

MRS. HOLDEN.

Grate the rough, dark places from the orange, quarter the orange, put the peel in weak salt and water 2 hours, boil in plenty of soft water till tender, scrape the juice and pulp from skin and seeds, cut the peel in thin, long slices; 1 pound of sugar for 1 pound of orange. Boil 20 minutes or longer.

PEACH PRESERVES.—(VERY RICH).

Use large, white clingstones, pare and remove the stones. To every pound of peaches, allow ½ of a pound of sugar. Make a thin syrup, boil the peaches in the syrup till tender, but not till they break. Put them into a bowl and pour the syrup over them. Put them in a dry, cool place and let them stand 2 days. Then make a new, rich syrup, allowing ¾ of a pound of sugar to one of fruit. Drain the peaches from the first syrup and boil them till they are clear in the second syrup.

WATERMELON RIND PRESERVES.

Cover the bottom and sides of the kettle with vine leaves. Put in a layer of rind and then a layer of vine leaves. In each layer put a small piece of alum, cover with leaves, then put a wet towel over the top, and water enough to cover them well. Let then simmer an hour. Then take them out on a dish and make a syrup of a pound of sugar and a pint of water, to a pound of rind. When the scum has stopped rising, put in the fruit and let it simmer a half hour. Take out the rind on a dish and let the syrup simmer an hour, then put in the fruit and simmer another half hour, then take it out and let stand until morning, then pour off the syrup and boil until thick as honey, and pour over the rind in a jar. Season with mace, ginger, or whatever you prefer.

ICES, CREAMS, JELLIES, ETC.

Custards for supper and an endless host of other such ladylike luxuries."—*Shelly.*

"*Sweet to the sense and lovely to the eye.*"

APPLE ICE.
MRS. RAMSEY.

Take fresh stewed apples that look white, run them through a sieve. To 1 teacupful of the sauce take 6 tablespoons of sugar and the whites of two eggs beaten to a stiff froth. Beat all together with a fork, flavor with lemon.

AMBER CREAM.
MRS. ROSSETER.

Soak ½ box of gelatine in 1 quart of milk 10 minutes. Let it come to a boil and stir in the yolks of 6 eggs beaten with 7 heaping tablespoons of powdered sugar. Cook until like soft custard. When it has been off the stove just 5 minutes, put in the beaten whites, flavor and mould.

BOHEMIAN CREAM.

Four ounces of any kind of fruit passed through a sieve. After sweetening, 1½ ounces isinglass dissolved to ½ pint fruit, 1 pint of rich cream whipped.

BEVIVO.
MRS. F. F. OLDHAM.

One-half box gelatine, 1 pint boiling water, 1 teacup sugar. Flavor with vanilla. 3 pints rich cream, whipped.

BAVARIAN CREAM.
MRS. PIERCE.

Soak ½ box of gelatine in a cup of cold water. Boil 1 pint of cream or rich milk and 11 tablespoonfuls of sugar. Blanch and roll ¾ of a pound of almonds. Pour the hot milk over them and when cool add the gelatine, flavor with vanilla, add 1 pint of whipped cream last. For peach or strawberry cream omit the vanilla and almonds and add 1 teacupful of fruit cooked as thick as marmalade, and use only ½ cup of sugar.

BANANA ICE CREAM.

MRS. E. G. BRIGHAM.

One pint of milk, 1 pint of cream, 2 eggs, 1 coffeecup of sugar, vanilla to taste. Beat the eggs till frothy, add the sugar gradually and then stir till eggs and sugar are thoroughly mixed. Lastly add milk and cream. Stir all well before placing in the freezer. When the cream is half frozen add 3 bananas finely cut with a silver knife. For peach cream leave out the eggs and use 1 can of peaches rubbed through a fine colander or sieve. Mix with the cream and freeze.

CURRANT ICE.

One pint of currant juice, 1 pound of sugar, 1 pint of water. Mix well, and when partly frozen add the whites of 3 eggs well beaten.

CHARLOTTE RUSSE.

MRS. REBECCA JOHNSON.

Dissolve ½ box of Cox's gelatine in 1 coffee cup of new milk; when thoroughly dissolved add 1 coffee cup of sugar. Place upon the stove and stir until the sugar is dissolved—do not let it cook, merely heat it, until the mixture is smooth. Then let it cool but not stiffen; into this stir 1 pint of cream, which has been whipped to a stiff froth, add lastly the beaten whites of 7 eggs. Chopped almonds.

CHARLOTTE RUSSE.

MRS. W. G. WAY.

One pint of thick cream beaten to a stiff froth; ½ box Cox's gelatine, dissolved in enough cold water to cover it. Heat 1 gill of milk and pour it over the gelatine; add 1 cup of pulverized sugar, 1 tablespoonful of vanilla, whites of 2 eggs beaten to a stiff froth. Stir all well together, and pour over a mould lined with sponge cake. Set in a cool place to harden.

CHARLOTTE RUSSE.

MRS. H. WHITNEY.

Mix with the yolks of 4 eggs ¼ pound sugar, ½ pint new milk; put it over the fire until it thickens like custard; do not let it boil. Soak

Ices, Creams, Jellies, Etc.

½ box of gelatine in a little water and add it. Put in a pan placed on ice a pint of very rich cream, flavored. When cold whip it. Pour the cream into another dish and put the custards into the pan on ice. Stir it until it becomes like jelly, then add cream very lightly. Line a dish with sponge cake; pour in the Charlotte and put on ice.

CHARLOTTE RUSSE.

MRS. M. P. WELLS.

One quart cream, 3 tablespoons Cox's gelatine; let the gelatine dissolve on the stove in a little of the cream; not too hot. Season the rest of the cream pretty sweet with sugar and flavor with vanilla. Whip the cream to a stiff froth, stir in the gelatine. Line a glass dish with pieces of sponge cake and pour over the cream. Prepare in the morning for tea.

CHARLOTTE RUSSE—No. 2.

One ounce Cooper's isinglass or Cox's gelatine, soak about an hour in a pint of milk, place over the fire until dissolved; add ½ pound sugar, and flavor with vanilla. Whip 1 quart cream. Remove the froth as it rises to a large bowl. Stir the dissolved isinglass, etc., until it begins to cool and thicken, then mix with the whipped cream. Beat all well and pour into moulds lined with sponge cake or with lady fingers.

CHARLOTTE RUSSE.—(GOOD).

MRS. CAROLINE BUTLER.

One-third of a box of Cox gelatine soaked for 1 hour, in 1 pint of cold milk, place over the fire and stir till dissolved, then add ½ pound of sugar. Flavor to taste with vanilla. 1 quart of cream whipped (with egg beater), removing to another bowl the froth as it rises. Stir the gelatine and milk, till it is cool and begins to thicken, mix with whipped cream, beat all together and pour into mould. (Should be prepared the day before using, unless cooled on ice).

CHOCOLATE BLANC MANGE.

MRS. ROSSETER.

One box of gelatine dissolved in 1 cup of milk, 3 heaping tablespoons grated chocolate. Boil 2 quarts of milk, sweeten to taste, add chocolate and gelatine. Pour into moulds and cool. Eat with sugar and cream.

CHOCOLATE BLANC MANGE.

MRS. JOHN EATON.

One quart of milk, 1 package of Cox's gelatine soaked in 1 cup of the milk 1 hour, 4 heaping tablespoons of grated chocolate wet with a little of the milk, 3 eggs beaten separately, ¾ of a cup of sugar, 2 teaspoons of vanilla. Boil the milk, stir in gelatine. Beat sugar and yolks together, add chocolate. Stir into this mixture, spoonful by spoonful of scalded milk and gelatine. Return to saucepan, stirring steadily till it almost boils. Remove from fire. Beat whites to a stiff meringue and stir in saucepan. Pour into moulds. Serve with cream and sugar. This quantity is sufficient for 12 people.

COFFEE CREAM.

MISS ELEANOR HAWKS.

One pint of milk, ½ box (scant) gelatine, 1½ ounce ground coffee, ½ pint rich cream, 2 eggs, ¾ cups sugar. Dissolve gelatine in ½ pint of milk, put the coffee in the other half, let it stand 1 hour, then steam coffee in milk 10 minutes, add gelatine and sugar beaten with the yolks, strain through fine muslin. When it begins to stiffen, beat the cream and whites of eggs separately, then add to the mixture. Pour into a mould and when cold it is ready for use. Chocolate can be used as a substitute for coffee, in which case 2 tablespoons of grated chocolate is sufficient.

CARAMEL JELLY.

MISS ELEANOR HAWKS.

A delightful addition to baked custard.

Three-fourth cup granulated sugar, ⅓ box gelatine, 1 large pint water, 6 drops almond extract. Soak the gelatine in ½ pint water 30 minutes. Let the other half be boiling hot on the stove. Melt the sugar in a small pan, *without water*, stir constantly. When it boils and is of a rich amber color, stir very slowly into the boiling water, add gelatine and water, strain, flavor and pour into a bowl. When the custard is baked and cold, turn it on a platter, and pile the jelly around it. If the custard is baked in a square pan, it will look much prettier when turned out.

COFFEE JELLY.

MRS. RAMSEY.

Soak one-half paper of gelatine in just enough tepid water to cover it. Take 1 scant pint of milk, put it on in a double boiler, and just before it comes to a boil stir in 4 well beaten eggs and ⅔ of a cup of sugar (beaten together). Do not let it boil only scald, until it becomes a little thick. Take from the fire and put in the dissolved gelatine, and 1½ cup of very strong coffee, which has been previously boiled and settled, pour into moulds to cool. In very warm weather use a little more gelatine, to insure its being hard enough. To be eaten with cream and sugar.

COFFEE JELLY.

MRS. PROF. MITCHELL.

Two-third box gelatine soaked till soft in 1 pint cold water, 1 quart strong hot coffee poured into this and sweetened to taste. Mould. Eat with sugar and cream.

CORN STARCH BLANC MANGE.

MISS VIRGINIA S. NYE.

One pint milk, 2 heaping tablespoons corn starch, ½ teacup sugar (scant), whites of 3 eggs. Dissolve corn starch in a little cold milk and stir into the boiling milk with the sugar. When it is quite thick stir in the well beaten whites. Flavor and pour into a mould.

Soak ½ box of gelatine in a quart of milk 1 hour. Put on the fire and stir as it warms. Take the 3 yolks and beat with a small cup of sugar. Add to the scalding milk stirring to the boiling point. Season with lemon or vanilla. Strain into a mould.

FROZEN FRUIT CUSTARD.

One pint of rich milk, 1 pint of cream whipped, yolks of 3 eggs, 1½ cupfuls of sugar, 1 pint of fresh peaches cut into small pieces, or fresh ripe berries. Beat the whites and sugar well together. Heat the pint of milk almost to the boiling point and add it gradually to the beaten eggs and sugar, return to the kettle and stir constantly until it has slightly thickened. When the custard is partly frozen, add the whipped cream, stir a few minutes longer and then stir in the fruit.

ICE CREAM—PEACH.

MRS. MORRIS, CINCINNATI.

One quart of rich cream, 1 pint of new milk, 1 cup of sugar, 1 large spoonful of gelatine, dissolve in a little of the milk. Heat the milk and stir in the gelatine and sugar, add the cream and 2 quarts of yellow peaches, and 1 cup of sugar mashed together with a fork.

ICE CREAM.—Perfect.
SOUTH CH. COOK BOOK.

One quart of cream, 1 quart of milk, 1 pint of sugar, ¼ of a box of Cox's gelatine and flour to taste. Dissolve the gelatine in 1 pint of milk on the back of the stove and add the other ingredients. No boiling necessary.

MRS. OGBURN'S ICE CREAM.

Four-fifths cream to one-fifth milk, 1 heaping teaspoon of gelatine to each quart, dissolve the gelatine in milk, flavor with vanilla.

ITALIAN CREAM.
MRS. NAHUM WARD.

Soak in cold water a little more than ½ a box of Cox's gelatine until soft. Scald a quart of milk in a bucket set in hot water, stir the gelatine into the milk until dissolved. Beat the yolks of 8 eggs with a little sugar and stir into the milk, and let it cook a little, but not till it curdles. Flavor with almonds and turn into a mould, wet with cold water. Let it stand 10 hours before using.

ICED APPLES.
MISS MARY SLACK, KY.

Pare and core nice cooking apples, make very sweet, put into a pan with a little water, cover closely, and stew rapidly on top of the stove until thoroughly cooked. Place them in a baking dish. Make a nice icing and put over thick. Set it in the stove and brown lightly. When cold serve with thick cream.

CARO DANA'S LEMON ICE.

From 8 to 10 lemons. Sugar more than for lemonade. 2 quarts water. Let the lemon peel stand in whilst you cool it on ice, then strain and freeze.

OAKLAND FROZEN LEMONADE.
MRS. G. M. WOODBRIDGE.

To 1 quart of rich lemonade add the well beaten whites of 6 eggs. Mix them well and freeze the mixture.

LEMON ICE.

Five lemons, 4 cups of sugar, 1½ quarts of water, 1 large tablespoon of gelatine dissolved in a little water. When almost frozen add the whites of 2 eggs beaten stiff, then finish freezing.

LEMON JELLY.

One-half box of gelatine, the peel and juice of 2 lemons. Let it stand over night in 1 pint of cold water, then add 1 pint of boiling water and 1 pint of sugar. Stir till all is dissolved, then pour into a mould.

LEMON JELLY.
MRS. COLLIER.

One box of gelatine, 1 pint of cold water, 3 lemons, squeeze these, cut up the peel and soak these in the gelatine an hour, add a pound of sugar, pour over this 1 quart of boiling water, strain and cool.

LEMON JELLY.

One Box Cox's gelatine soaked in 1 pint cold water. When dissolved add 1 quart boiling water, in 1 pint of which, some sticks of cinnamon have been boiled. 1½ pounds (2 pints) of sugar, juice of 4 lemons. Strain through fine tin strainer.

LEMON CREAM.

Eggs 3, beat the yolks with the juice of 3 lemons, 1 cup sugar. Set it at the back of your range, or in a pan of boiling water and stir until it becomes thick, then pour it into a dish, whip the whites to a stiff froth, use the juice of 1 lemon and a spoonful of sugar to flavor with, heap this over the cream and serve.

LEMON BUTTER.
C. D. BLYMYER.

Three lemons, outside and juice, 6 eggs, 1 pint sugar, butter size of an egg. Beat the lemons, sugar and eggs together. Put the butter in a kettle and when hot add the lemons, etc. Stir until it commences to blubber, then it is done.

MACEDONIAN JELLY.
MRS. M. D. FOLLETT.

Let 2 ounces of gelatine dissolve in 3 pints of cold water, set for half an hour on the fire and melt gradually, add the juice of 4 lemons, 12 spoonfuls of sugar, and stir in the well beaten whites of 2 eggs, over a slow fire. As soon as it boils throw in a large spoonful of cold water. Skim the froth from the top, and strain through a wet flannel jelly-bag. Cool a little of this jelly in a mould, and place on ice. As soon as set, add Malaga grapes removed from the stem, add another layer of jelly, then grapes, repeating the process till the mould is full, having a layer of jelly on top. While the layers are cooling, keep the rest of the jelly warm on the fire. Instead of grapes, small pieces of pine-apple may be used, or the kernels of English walnuts in halves.

MOONSHINE.

MRS. G. W. WAY.

Beat the whites of 6 eggs in a broad plate to a stiff froth. Then add gradually 6 tablespoonfuls of powdered sugar. To make it thicker use more sugar up to a pint. Beat in about 1 heaping tablespoonful of preserved peaches, cut in tiny bits, or 1 cup of jelly. Set on ice until thoroughly chilled. In serving pour in each saucer some rich cream flavored and sweetened. On the cream place some of the moonshine.

NEAPOLITAN BLANC MANGE.

MRS. EATON.

One box gelatine, 3 pints of milk, a pinch of salt. Put the gelatine into the milk and boil up once. Sweeten to taste. Divide into 4 parts. One part flavor with vanilla, 2nd part beat together with yolks. Steam till melted 1 little square of chocolate and pour 3d part of milk and gelatine over this. Fourth part tint with cochineal. Flavor as you wish. Wait until almost cold, then pour in mould each layer, one on the other. Set away until cold and hardened.

ORANGE JELLY.

MRS. S. N. LOVELL.

Peel and cut up 6 oranges, sugar well, ½ box of gelatine, ½ pint cold water, soak 1 hour. 1½ pints boiling water, sugar and flavor with 2 lemons and stick cinnamon, color with burnt sugar. Pour over oranges.

ORANGE SPONGE.

MRS. H. C. EVANS.

One pound of sugar in a bowl, 6 good sized oranges, squeeze, and stir the juice on sugar. Dissolve 3½ sheets of Cooper's isinglass in water. Add this to the sugar. Juice of 1½ lemons, drop in the whites of 3 eggs well beaten. Beat all together till it is thick and frothy. Put in a shape, and set on ice.

PEACH JELLY.

Dissolve in sufficient water, 1 ounce of isinglass, strain it. Halve 12 large peaches and pare them. Make a syrup of 1 pound sugar and a half pint of water. Into this put the fruit and kernels, boil gently

15 minutes, then place the fruit on a plate, and cook the syrup 10 minutes longer. Add to it the juice of 3 lemons and the isinglass. A pyramid mould is pretty for this. Fill part full of jelly, and when set, put in ½ of the peaches. Let it harden, and then add more jelly and so on. Base of mould be of jelly.

PINE-APPLE JELLY.
MRS. JOHN NEWTON.

Four large tablespoonfuls of Cox's gelatine, 1 pint of water, 1 large cup of sugar, juice of 2 lemons. Make it scalding hot and strain. While cooling stir in ½ can of grated pine-apple.

RUSSIA CREAM.
MRS. DR. WOODBRIDGE, BELLAIRE, O.

Four eggs, 1 cup of sugar, 1 quart of milk, ½ box gelatine dissolved in ½ pint of warm water. Beat the yolks of eggs and sugar together, and cook with the milk like custard. Take from the fire and add the well beaten whites of the eggs, stirring rapidly for a few minutes. Add the gelatine, then a teaspoonful of vanilla. Pour into a mould to harden. Turn out upon a platter and cut off in blocks as in ice cream. Make this the day before.

SCORCHED CREAM.
MISS MARTHA PUTNAM.

One quart sweet milk, 3 eggs, 6 ounces sugar, 3 tablespoonfuls flour. Bring the milk to a boil, and stir in the ingredients. Boil all together two or three minutes. Pour into a deep dish, and sprinkle sugar over the top, and scorch with a very hot flat-iron. Eaten cold, is nice to eat with ripe currants or any small fruit.

TAPIOCA AND PEACHES.
MRS. H. C. EVANS.

One cup tapioca soaked, when soft add 1 cup sugar, and cook in water till tender. When done stir in canned peaches. Put in mould. Eat cold with cream.

TAPIOCA CREAM.
MISS IRISH.

Two tablespoonfuls of tapioca, wash, and soak 2 hours. Put in a quart of boiling milk and cook ½ hour. Beat the yolks of 4 eggs with a little sugar, add, and cook three minutes longer. Beat the whites to a stiff froth, take the pudding from the fire and stir in flavoring and beaten whites. Serve cold.

PIES, PASTRY, ETC.

" Compounded of many simples."

MOTHER'S APPLE PIE.

MRS. H. B. SHIPMAN.

Roll out the paste to fit the pie-plate and fill with early Chandlers, pared and quartered. Cover with a rich crust. Do not press the edges together, but trim them off evenly. Bake about ¾ of an hour. When done, remove the top crust carefully, mash the apple fine and season with a cup of sugar, small piece of butter and a little nutmeg. Sift powdered sugar over the top. Serve the day it is baked.

APPLE MINUTE PIE.

MRS. A. T. NYE.

To be made of the early summer apples.

Line and cover pie-plate with pastry, sprinkling flour between, that they may be separated. Stew and season early Chandlers, and fill the pies after baking the crusts. To be eaten the same day.

APPLE TART.

MRS. ROSSETER.

Make crust enough for two pies. Peel and cut your apples and fill the dish (no under crust). Bake till the apples are soft, and crust brown. Take off the crust, turn upside down on plate. While the apple is hot, break and stir in an egg, a lump of butter, and 3 spoonfuls cream. Sweeten pretty sweet, add cinnamon. Eat with cream.

CHOPPED APPLE PIE.

Chop apples fine, 2 eggs, 1 cup of sugar, or till sweet enough, 1 cup cream. Bake without upper crust.

CUSTARD PIE.

MRS. H. C. EVANS.

One pint of milk, 3 eggs, saving out 2 whites. Beat the eggs with 2 tablespoonfuls flour and sugar to taste. Scald the milk in a bucket set in boiling water. Stir in eggs and flour and let cook until thick. Season with lemon and put in crusts previously baked. Beat the 2 whites with about a half cup of sugar, and pour over top. Set in the oven a few moments to harden.

COCOANUT PIE.

MRS. ROSSETER.

One grated cocoanut, 1 pound sugar, ½ pound butter, 6 eggs. Beat sugar and eggs as for cake, then mix in eggs and cocoanut. No upper crust. Makes 3 pies.

COCOANUT PIE.

MRS. DR. SAM'L. HART.

Two eggs, 4 tablespoons of sugar, 1 coffee cup of grated cocoanut, 1 pint of milk, 1 tablespoon of corn starch, a small piece of butter. Bake with one crust.

PUMPKIN OR SQUASH PIE.

Cook well and strain. To 3 pints of pumpkin add 2 eggs, 2 cups of sugar, 1 teaspoon of ginger, 1 teaspoon of cinnamon, 1 tablespoon of butter, then 1 quart of sweet milk.

CHOCOLATE PIE.

MRS. C. S. HALL.

Yolks of 2 eggs, 3 tablespoons of corn starch, 4 tablespoons of chololate, 6 tablespoons of sugar. Mix all together and stir into a pint of boiling water. Make the crust and bake first. Beat the whites and put on top when baked.

CREAM PIE.

MRS. CAROLINE D. DAWES.

Three cups of rich cream, sweeten to suit taste, 1 small tablespoon of flour, a little salt and nutmeg.

ORANGE CREAM PIE.
MISS IRISH.

Beat thoroughly the yolks of 2 eggs with 1 cup of sugar, add 1 small tablespoonful of flour and 1 small tablespoon of corn starch (dissolved in a little milk), pour into 1 pint of boiling milk and let it cook about 3 minutes, flavor with extract of orange and pour into a baked crust. Beat the whites with 2 tablespoons of sugar, flavor with orange, spread on top, and slightly brown in the oven.

CREAM PIE.
MRS. SLACK.

One pint of cream, 3 tablespoons of sugar, 1 tablespoon of flour, a little nutmeg, white of 1 egg—*not* beaten separately but stirred thoroughly with the flour and sugar. Bake with 2 crusts. Bake slowly, keeping a place open in the upper crust to let the steam escape.

MOTHER FAY'S CREAM PIES.—1800.

One quart of cream, 1½ cups of sugar, whites of 2 eggs well beaten, 2 teacups of stoned raisins, nutmeg. Stir well together. This will fill 2 large deep pudding dishes. Line the dish with pastry, (not too short) pour in ½ the above, wetting the crust around the edge, then add upper crust and prick. Bake slow and eat cold.

CREAM PIE.
MRS. M. SIMPSON, CRAWFORDSVILLE, IND.

One and one-half pints of sweet milk, 1 tablespoonful of flour, 1½ teacups of sugar, 1 tablespoon of butter, 3 eggs, flavor to taste. Boil the milk and stir in the yolks and ½ of the sugar and flour well beaten together, then the butter. Have the crust pricked to prevent blistering and then bake it. When baked add the custard. Set it in the oven a few moments. Beat the whites to a froth, with the rest of the sugar. Spread this on the pie and brown it slightly.

LEMON PIE.
MRS. PROF. BEACH.

One lemon cut in 1 cup of cold water. Heat slowly and simmer a few minutes. Strain out the rinds and seeds, pressing all the juice out. Add 1 cup of sugar and 1 tablespoonful of corn starch dissolved in cold water. Cook this till it thickens, and then add the beaten yolks of 2 eggs. Bake the crust separately, fill it with the mixture. Beat the whites stiff with 1 teaspoonful of sugar. Spread on top and brown.

LEMON PIE.

MRS. C. S. HALL.

One cup of sugar, ⅔ cup of water, 3 tablespoonfuls of flour, 1 piece of butter size of an egg. Grate the rind of 1 lemon, slice the inside very thin and lay in the bottom of the pan, before putting the custard in. If the lemon is good this will make 2 pies. Make crust the same as for custard pie.

LEMON CUSTARD PIE.

MRS. WELLS.

The juice and grated rind of 2 lemons, ½ teacup butter, 4 spoonfuls cream, 6 eggs, 3 cups sugar, ½ pint milk. The lemons, yolks, and butter beaten together, then add sugar, whites and cream. 3 pies.

MRS. GOV. MEIGS'S MINCE PIE—1830.

DAPHNE C. SQUIRES.

Three pounds of beef, parboiled, 2¾ pounds suet, 9 pounds apples, 2½ pounds sugar, 4 tablespoons salt, 2 tablespoons fine pepper, 1 tablespoon cloves, 2 tablespoons mace, 1½ tablespoon cinnamon, 1 pint of boiled cider, or syrup of fruit.

MINCE PIES.

MRS. EDGERTON.

Three pounds beef, 2 pounds suet, 1 pound currants, 1 pound raisins, 1 pound citron, 4 pounds sugar, 4 quarts chopped apple, 1 pint raspberry jam, 1 quart boiled cider. Nutmeg, cloves, mace, also grated rind of lemon and orange and the juice of the lemon.

MINCE PIES.

MRS. E. S. McINTOSH.

One-third of meat from the neck of the beef, two-thirds of apples. 6 pounds of beef, 2 pounds fat pork, cook together and chop fine. Measure meat after chopping and add twice as much chopped apples, then add 1 pound suet chopped fine, 2 pounds raisins, 2 pounds dried currants, ½ pound citron, 2 nutmegs 1½ tablespoonfuls cinnamon, 6 pounds sugar. Pack when well mixed in jars and run suet over the top, when you want to use add cider, sweetened to taste and bake.

MINCE PIES.

MRS. I. R. WATERS.

Two pounds boiled and chopped meat, ¾ pound fat salt pork,

chopped fine, 2 pounds sugar, 1 cup molasses, 3 pounds apple, chopped fine, 1 pound currants, 3 pound raisins, ½ pound citron, 1 ounce cinnamon, 1 ounce cloves, 2 nutmegs. Make quite moist with boiled cider.

PUMPKIN PIE.

MRS. BARBER.

For 1 pie a full ½ pint of rich milk, 1 heaping tablespoonful of pumpkin, 1 egg, beat white and yellow separately, ½ teaspoon flour. Sugar to suit your taste. A little ginger, cinnamon, and nutmeg. Beat all well together, adding the whipped white of the egg last, which should be stirred in quickly, but thoroughly. Bake 15 or 20 minutes in a quick oven.

PUMPKIN PIE.

MRS. HILDRETH.

One quart stewed pumpkin, 3 pints of milk, 6 eggs, sugar, nutmeg, ginger, and other spices to your taste.

POTATO PIE.

MRS. H. FEARING.

One-fourth pound potatoes, 1 quart of milk, 3 tablespoons melted butter, 4 well beaten eggs, add sugar and flavoring to taste.

PEACH COBBLER.

MRS. REPPERT, SCOTT'S LANDING.

Take 1 quart of flour, 4 tablespoons of lard or butter, ½ teaspoon of salt, mix as for biscuit, either with sweet milk or water, roll thin and line a pudding dish or dripping pan. Mix 3 tablespoons of flour and 2 of sugar together and sprinkle over the crust, then put in layers 3 pints of thin sliced peaches, and now and then a slice of the crust. Sprinkle over them 1 coffee cup of sugar, wet the edges with a little flour and water mixed. Put on upper crust, press the edges together, make 2 openings in top an inch in length. Bake in quick oven half an hour. Serve with cream.

PUFF PASTE.

MRS. EDGERTON—MRS. BLISS.

Into 1 quart of flour stirr 1 teaspoonful of salt, if you intend to use butter as shortening. If you intend to use half butter and half lard stir in 2 teaspoons of salt. Cut ½ pound of shortening into the flour, but do not moisten the flour in stirring it in. With ½ tumbler of cold water wet the flour as lightly as possible to a stiff paste. Flour the moulding board and the rolling pin, roll out the paste to ½ an inch in thickness, cover it with ¼ of a pound of the shortening, cut in small bits, sprinkle with flour, roll it up into a long roll, flour it again, fold in the ends, and with the rolling pin floured, roll it out again to ½ an inch in thickness. Cover it with another pound of shortening and repeat the same process as before, then roll it out and use immediately.

PIE CRUST.

One teacup of lard, 3 teacups of flour, pinch of salt. Mix lard and flour together until fine, then add water to make proper consistency to roll. Don't work much.

PUFF PASTE.

MRS. ARIUS NYE.

Rub ½ a pound of butter into 1 pound of flour, whites of 4 eggs beaten, 2 ounces of loaf sugar.

PUFF PASTE.—Celebrated.

MRS. JEROME BUCKINGHAM.

One pound of flour, 1 pound of butter, 1 egg. Mix the flour and a lump of butter or lard, size of an egg, and the egg to a very stiff paste with cold water. Knead well for 10 or 15 minutes; divide the butter into 6 equal parts, squeeze the buttermilk all out of the butter. Roll the paste and spread on 1 part of the butter, dredging it with flour. Repeat until all of the butter is rolled in.

PIE CRUST.

MISS CUTHBERT.

One pint of flour, heaping tablespoon of lard, a little water, spread the dough and roll the butter into the crust, a little salt.

"RHUBARB takes all flavors and gives none, therefore, it helps to make up a deficiency of a more costly material."

Wash your rhubarb, mince it fine, sweeten it and bake it until soft, when cold stir in raspberries or other fruit, and make into pies

PIE PLANT PIE.

MRS. G. M. WOODBRIDGE.

One cup of stewed pie plant, 1 cup of sugar, yolks of 3 eggs, white of 1 egg, dissolve 1 spoon of butter, flavor with lemon. Bake in a bottom crust. Make meringue of the whites of 2 eggs. Lay this over the top and brown slightly.

Some bake the crust separately, and putting the pie plant, sugar, etc. together, set it in hot water, and stir, and cook, and then put it into the crust and add meringue.

PEACH TART.
MRS. H. WHITNEY.

Line a baking dish with pastry and after baking, fill with cut peach preserves. Cover with whipped cream.

SQUASH PIE.
MRS. J. H. PARSONS, COLUMBUS, OHIO.

One-half pint of stewed and sifted squash, 1 egg, a piece of butter the size of an egg, $\frac{1}{2}$ cup of sugar, $\frac{1}{2}$ pint of sweet milk, $\frac{1}{2}$ teaspoon each of nutmeg and cinnamon, and a pinch of salt. Beat all together but the milk, then add the milk. Bake in a deep pie dish $\frac{3}{4}$ of an hour.

STRAWBERRY RICE MOUNTAIN.
MRS. R. M. HILL.

Cook rice as for ordinary use, (rather stiff), spread a large flat plate with rice, then a layer of strawberries, then rice, then strawberries, forming a pyramid having a large strawberry on top. It will add greatly to the appearance to have a row of the nicest berries carefully and evenly arranged around the edge. Make in the morning and eat cold with sugar and cream.

STRAWBERRY SHORT CAKE.
HOUSEKEEPER'S FRIEND.

Take 3 pints of flour, 1$\frac{1}{2}$ cups of shortening, (part lard and part butter) 1 teaspoon of salt, 1 cup of cold water. Cream the shortening until very light, drop through the flour, add the salt, then sprinkle the water in Turn it out on a pastry board, mix it a little with a broad knife, then gently pound with a rolling pin until ready to roll out, roll nearly a half inch in thickness, cut in long squares or put in round pie pans and bake quickly. As soon as it is done split open, butter the inside of both pieces and sugar liberally, then put a layer of berries on the under crust and sugar, place the top crust on and sugar the top well. It takes 3 pints of berries.

SYRUP FOR SAME.—One pint of berries, $\frac{1}{2}$ pint of sugar. Boil 10 minutes, strain and cool. Pour this over when you serve if you like.

CANDIES.

"Sweetmeats, messengers of strong prevailment in unhardened youth."—*Shakespeare.*

For all candy making it is important to have suitable kettles to boil in. Copper or porcelain lined are the best; iron will discolor the candy. Use a gas or coal oil stove as the heat can be better regulated. Granulated sugar is best. Candy should not be stirred while boiling. Cream of Tartar should not be added till the syrup is boiling. Butter should be put in when candy is almost done. Flavoring is best put in when candy is poured in the plates to cool.

AMBER CANDY.
MRS. WOODRUFF.

Two cups sugar, 1 cup vinegar. Boil but not stir until it crisps in cold water, turn on buttered pans, thin. When cold break and eat.

BUTTER SCOTCH.

One cup sugar, 1 cup molasses, 1 tablespoonful sweet milk, 1 tablespoonful essence lemon, butter size of an egg.

CREAM CANDY.

Two pounds coffee sugar, 1 teacup water, 4 teaspoonfuls vinegar, 1 teaspoonful butter, 2 teaspoonfuls vanilla. Do not stir, and do not cook too long. Dry by dropping in cold water.

CHOCOLATE CARAMELS.
MISS M. HARTE.

Two cups of brown sugar, ¼ cup of water, 2 tablespoons of vinegar, a small piece of butter, boil 10 minutes and then put ½ cup of chocolate in the mixture, pour on buttered plates, when cool cut in squares.

CHOCOLATE DROPS.

MISS M. HARTE.

Four cups of confectioner's sugar, 1 cup of cream (flavoring), boil 6 minutes, beat till cool, when cool mould, and roll in 1 cake of melted chocolate. The creams of English Walnuts may be made in the same way.

(PARLOR) ENGLISH WALNUTS.

MISS M. HARTE.

Take equal amount of egg and water in 2 tumblers of the same size, put in enough confectioner's sugar to stiffen, flavor with vanilla, press in squares and put a piece of english Walnut on top.

CREAM FIGS.

Wash and open the figs and put a ball of cream (such as used for chocolate drops) inside each fig.

FRUIT CANDY.

MRS. C. D. BLYMYER.

Two pounds coffee sugar, 2 pounds almonds blanched and split, 1 pound raisins stoned, ½ pound figs, cut size of almonds, ¼ pound citron, teacup of cream, butter size of an egg. Mix with a little water as if making starch, add butter, cream and vanilla. Boil until it begins to thicken, then put in the fruit and stir until creamed and white. Pour into wet napkin and roll up as if a boiled dumplin. Do not eat until entirely cold. It will slice like fruit cake.

LEMON CANDY.

MRS. BARBER.

One pound sugar, 1 cup water. Boil slowly ½ hour, clear with a little hot vinegar. Test by dropping into water, and when brittle, flavor strongly with lemon. Pour into buttered tins and when cool mark off into squares.

MOLASSES CANDY.

MRS. W. W. MILLS.

One quart of molasses, ½ cup of vinegar, 1 cup of sugar, butter the size of an egg, 1 teaspoonful of soda dissolved in hot water and stirred in just before removing from the fire, flavor to taste. When sufficiently cool pull until white.

Candies.

NUT CANDY.

MISS MAY WOODRUFF.

Five cups of sugar, 6 tablespoons of water, 4 tablespoons of vinegar, 1 tablespoon butter. Boil (without stirring) till it crisps in cold water. Line buttered pans with peanuts and pour the candy over them. When nearly cold mark off into squares.

NUT CANDY.

MRS. W. W. MILLS.

Three cups of brown sugar, ½ cup of vinegar, ½ cup of water, butter the size of an egg. Test in cold water. When done pour over a buttered plate that has been lined with hickory kernels.

ORANGE BON-BONS.

Sprinkle enough orange juice into a cup with confectioner's sugar to make of right consistency to mould into any desired shape, then roll in granulated sugar and place on buttered paper.

PEPPERMINTS.

Mix thoroughly in a tin cup 1 tumblerful of confectioner's sugar with 8 teaspoons of cold water and flavor with peppermint. Place the tin cup with its mixture in a pan of boiling water and let it boil 3 minutes, then drop it from a teaspoon on to buttered paper. Color pink with cochineal.

TAFFY.

MISS BARBER.

Two cups of molasses, 1 cup of brown sugar, butter size of an egg, 1 tablespoon vinegar, add last a pinch of soda. Put all together in a kettle and boil twenty minutes. Cool in shallow tins and then pull.

WHITE TAFFY.

Two pounds granulated sugar, 1 teacup cold water, 2 teaspoons vinegar, 2 teaspoons butter. Boil without stirring till brittle when tested in water. When done add 1 tablespoon vanilla and pour on buttered platter to cool. Pull rapidly till white and brittle. Cut into sticks.

FRENCH CANDIES.

MARY HART.

One and a half pound of confectioner's sugar mixed thoroughly with ½ of a cocoanut grated. Add enough water to make a stiff dough. Put this on a candy board (a bread board will answer the purpose) knead in more sugar and divide into 4 parts. Take 1 part and before moulding into balls mix in ½ of 5 cts. worth of cochineal (liquid) into ½ of this. Mould all this into balls and put a pink ball on top of a white one. With another part get 5 cts. worth of dates and seed them. Place a ball of cocoanut cream between each date. With the third part take ½ of a cake of chocolate melted and roll the cocoanut balls into this. With the fourth part get 5 cts. worth of both almonds and English walnuts. Take out the meats of both and place a meat on each ball.

HONEY CANDY.

MARY M. HART.

One cup of honey, 1 cup of sugar, ¼ of a cup of water, a small piece of butter. Boil till brittle when tested in water. Pull while cooling.

HICKORY NUT CANDY.

MARY M. HART.

Two cups of sugar, ½ cup of water. Boil till brittle. Flavor with vanilla. Have 1 cup full of hickory nut meats. Spread on a buttered plate and pour the candy over the nuts. When cool cut in squares.

VINEGAR CANDY.

MARY M. HART.

Two cups of sugar, ½ cup of water, ½ cup of vinegar, 1 teaspoon of lemon, a small piece of butter. Boil till brittle. Pull white.

FIG CANDY.

MARY M. HART.

One cup of sugar, ¼ cup of water, ¼ tablespoonful of cream tartar. Don't stir while boiling. Just before taking from the fire, stir in cream tartar. Wash the figs, open and lay in a tin pan. When the candy is brittle, pour over the figs.

PEANUT CANDY.

MARY M. HART.

Two cups of sugar, ½ cup of water. When boiling add 1 teaspoonful cream tartar dissolved in a little water. Cook until brittle when dropped in cold water. Butter the size of a hickory nut. Have peanuts shelled and on a buttered plate. Pour candy over. When cool cut in squares.

CANDIED HOARHOUND.—PURE.

MARY M. HART.

Boil hoarhound, 10 cts. worth, in water until juice is all extracted, take 1 cup of sugar and water, when boiled to a feather add hoarhound juice. Boil again till brittle. Pour on a plate dusted with fine sugar. Cut in sticks. This is good for a cold, being pure.

BUTTER AND CHEESE.

" She brought forth butter in a lordly dish."

TO MAKE A NO. 1 BUTTER.
JAMES WEST.

In order to make a number one grade of butter, have no stagnant ponds or mudholes in the pasture, but perfectly pure water for the cows to drink, and clean, dry quarters for the cows to lie in. Scald the milk buckets at least once a day, in short, thoroughly scald *all* the vessels used about the milk. Strain and keep it in a room or cellar kept for that purpose only. (Milk and butter take up the odors thrown off from vegetables or even the unavoidable mould that generates in a common cellar or room used for storing any and everything). Let the milk stand from 24 to 36 hours before skimming. When enough cream is gathered for a churning, bring it to 62° by putting the jars on ice. When churned, work as much of the milk out as you can, and salt 1 ounce to the pound. After working in salt, set by in a cool place a few hours, then thoroughly work and roll. Never use the paddle with a sliding motion, nor slick it over the butter while rolling, or after, as a sliding motion breaks the grain and makes the butter oily. Manage to have the butter come solid, then there will be no trouble in having a nice roll that will keep its shape. But butter churned soft and hardened up with ice or in other ways, will not keep its shape and more than likely will become rancid in less than a week. To make butter in winter keep the milk where it will not freeze. Never set your cream by the fire to warm up and get ready to churn, rather set it in warm water until the right temperature is obtained, and scalding the churn until it is thoroughly warmed.

BUTTER.
MRS. WALDO PUTNAM.

To make good butter it is essential to have a room for butter and milk only, and to have it well ventilated. The old way is to set in *shallow pans.* Let it stand from 24 to 36 hours, (longer in winter), before skimming. Churn, salt, set it away. The next day work out *all* the buttermilk and make into rolls.

BUTTER.

MRS. G. S. MARSHALL.

I have practiced this way of making butter for 30 years. Have thoroughly cleansed stone crocks sunned and rinsed with cool water and set in a pure, well-ventilated cellar. Into them strain the milk and let stand uncovered for 24 hours. Skim cream in a jar which must be covered. As each skimming is added stir well the cream. This is to prevent the mould from forming on the top of the cream. Keep the cream in the coolest possible place, in a refrigerator, if you are fortunate enough to have one. I have an ice box. I use a stone churn with a wooden dasher and cover, and churn every other day in warm weather. If the cream has a temperature of 60° the butter will form in about 20 minutes. Have ready a wooden bowl and ladle which have been scalded and cooled. Into this put the butter as gathered. Wash 2 or 3 times in cold water and salt to taste. I use about 1 ounce to a pound. When it has stood 8 hours, work well. Make into rolls and sell for 20 cts. per pound.

CREAM CHEESE.

MRS. ISRAEL DEVOL.

Cream cheese made from Jersey milk. Set the milk at night in a cool place. In the morning take the thick cream off, strain morning milk into the same vessel, warm the milk to 90°, have the rennet prepared by soaking over night in salt and water. Put in 1 tablespoonful of rennet to a gallon of milk. If rennet is good it will bring it in 15 minutes. Let it set 10 minutes after it coagulates, then cut with a long knife both ways. Let stand for ½ hour, then stir gently every 10 minutes for 4 or 5 times. Put a thin cloth strainer over the basket or tub with holes in it. Take hold of two corners of cheese cloth, moving the curd, from one side to the other a few times, then let set a few minutes, turn again and twist up the cloth. Next take a knife and cut curd into inch squares, then twist up the cloth again. Keep at this every few minutes until dry enough to chop and salt ready for pressing, using ½ teaspoon of salt to 1 pound of curd. Put in hoop and put to press.

SICK ROOM.

It is a dangerous thing to constantly carry exercise to the fatigue point. Every woman should make *an inflexible* law of her life to lie down in the middle of the day at least fifteen minutes, closing the eyes and shutting off as far as possible all anxious thought.

In the recumbent position every muscle of the body is placed at perfect rest; all tension is removed from nerve centres.

BEEF TEA.

One pound of lean beef, 1 pint of water. Chop the meat and let it stand on ice over night, or several hours during the day. Boil 15 minutes. Some let it simmer slowly on the back of the range for 2 hours—then strain.

CREAM OF TARTAR BEVERAGE.

Two even spoonfuls of cream of tartar, 1 pint of boiling water, sweeten to taste, or,

One tumbler of cold water, 1 teaspoon of cream of tartar, 1 of sugar.

AN OLD-FASHIONED RECIPE FOR A LITTLE HOME COMFORT.

Take of thought for self one part, two parts of thought for family; equal parts of common sense and broad intelligence, a large modicum of the sense of fitness of things, a heaping measure of living above what your neighbors think of you, twice the quantity of keeping within your income, a sprinkling of what tends to refinement and æsthetic beauty, stirred thick with Christian principle of the true brand, and set it to rise.

DISINFECTANTS.

Copperas.—One pound of copperas dissolved in 1 quart of water will destroy the foulest smell.

Copperas.—One and one-half pounds dissolved in a gallon of water. Sixty pounds to a barrel of water.

SULPHUR TO DISINFECT A HOUSE.

For a room 10 feet square, 2 pounds of sulphur should be used. Shut your room tight, put your sulphur in an iron pan, set it on fire

For Sick Room.

with hot coals, sprinkled with a little saltpetre. Keep the room closed 12 hours. It would be well to set your pan upon bricks in a vessel of water.

ZINC SOLUTION.

Common sulphate of zinc and common salt, dissolved in water, 4 ounces of zinc, 2 ounces of salt, 1 gallon of water. Use this on bed linen, clothing, towels, etc., *boiling hot* if possible.

EXCELLENT DISINFECTANTS.

Fresh air—sun-light—hot water—flowing water, soap and a scrub brush—ventilation and cleanliness—the broom and the dust cloth.

DYSENTERY in its worst form has been cured by drinking wheat flour stirred in water to about the consistency of cream. You may add a pinch of salt. Good in cases of chronic diarrhœa.

FLAX SEED LEMONADE.

Four tablespoons of seed, 1 quart of boiling water, juice of 2 lemons, sweeten to taste. Steep 3 hours, if too thick add cold water with the lemon juice. Good for colds.

GEMS.—FOR DYSPEPTICS.

MRS. M. D. FOLLETT.

One cup of gluten flour, 1 cup of milk, 1 egg, 1 teaspoonful of baking powder, 1 tablespoonful or less of butter. Beat well and bake in hot gem-pans in a quick oven. Butter may be omitted.

Gluten flour is prepared from whole wheat and is nearly free from starch.

HOT MILK AS A RESTORATIVE.

Heat it as hot as it can be sipped. Take a goblet of it when fatigued in mind or body. It is cordial and reviving in its influence.

IN-GROWING TOE-NAILS.

Heat very hot a small piece of tallow in a spoon and pour it on the granulations. Pain and tenderness are relieved at once, and in a few days the edge of the nail is exposed so as to admit of being cut away.

MILK AND LIME WATER.

Take a lump of unslacked lime, put it in a glass bottle, add water until the lime is slacked and of the consistency of thick cream. The lime settles at the bottom leaving the water clear. Three or four tablespoons of this may be put to a goblet of milk and it will agree with any one.

MOSS LEMONADE.

One handful of Irish moss washed well in several waters. 1 quart of boiling water poured upon the moss and left to cool. Steep it for ½ an hour, sweeten and add the juice of 1 lemon.

OAT MEAL AND BEEF TEA.

Two tablespoonfuls of fine oat meal made perfectly smooth in 2 teaspoons of cold water. Put this into a pint of strong beef tea. Boil 8 minutes. Keep stirring all the time—if lumpy, strain.

MISCELLANEOUS.

"Who sweeps a room as for Thy law,
Makes that and th' action fine."
—*Herbert.*

BEEF GALL.

Get it fresh from your butcher. Use 1 tablespoon to a gallon of water. Put in a large tablespoon of salt, set in a cool place. Good for washing carpets, calicos, etc.

CEMENT FOR MAKING LEATHER BOOTS WATER PROOF.

Used for a century by New England fishermen.

Four ounces tallow, 1 ounce resin, 1 ounce beeswax. Melt together with a gentle heat and add equal bulk of Neat foot oil. Melt when used and rub in boots before the fire.

CLEANING FLUID.

MRS. GEO. DANA.

One gallon gasoline, 1 ounce alchohol, ¼ ounce bay rum, ¼ ounce spirits of ammonia, ¼ ounce chloroform, ¼ ounce ether, ¼ ounce powdered borax. Add more borax and more ammonia for badly soiled articles.

CORN STARCH PASTE.

Corn starch makes the best paste for scrap books. Dissolve a small quantity in cold water, then cook it thoroughly. Be careful not to get it too thick. When cold it should be thin enough to apply with a brush.

CLEAR STARCHING AND IRONING.—FRENCH SYSTEM.

White soap, Coleman's starch, 2 clean dusters, a soft cloth to use as a damper, an old raisin box with a layer of powdered bath brick collars, cuffs, shirts, etc., washed and dried but unstarched, a handful of dry starch in a bowl, ½ teaspoon of lump borax dissolved in a teacup of boiling water placed at one side of basin. Pour some cold water over the starch, a little at a time until the lumps are gone, then add the cup of borax water. It now has the consistency of good milk or thin cream. Take the piece of white soap and rub in the starch water as if washing, until it is quite pasty. Add a few drops of Paris blue dissolved. Take 6 collars for instance, dip them in cold water and wring them out. Then wash them in the starch water, wring them out and wash them as it were in the air. Then lay one by one in a clean cloth, wringing in the cloth. Have a hot iron, rub in the brick dust, dust with cloth. Have a piece of white wax in the layers of a clean cloth. Rub iron hastily over. Dust again. For a beginner 'tis best to lay a cloth over the collar first. An expert will dispense with this. Iron first on one side and then the other until the steam ceases to rise, then polish by bearing more heavily on the iron. Bring the two button hole ends together, dampen with the lips and press iron on the two ends. Hang the circled collar on a clean stick to dry.

EXCELLENT HAIR WASH.

Take 1 ounce of borax, ½ ounce of camphor; powder these ingredients fine, and dissolve them in 1 quart of boiling water. Damp the hair frequently. This wash cleanses and strengthens the hair. The camphor will form into lumps after being dissolved, but the water will be sufficiently impregnated.

LEAKING LAMPS.

If lamps be cleaned and wiped dry and the wicks turned down below the top of the burners, there will never be a trace of oil upon the outside.

MIXTURE FOR WASHING CARPETS.

MRS. ROLSTON.

One bar soap, 4 ounces borax, 8 ounces sal soda, 2 ounces alum. Boil in ½ gallon of water 15 minutes; add 4 gallons of water. Wash with this as much of the carpet as you can reach at once. Then take a smooth shingle and draw toward you, taking up all the lather into a bucket by itself. Then wash with clean water and clean cloths. Wipe as dry as possible with dry cloths, and proceed to another place.

SILVER CLEANER.

GORHAM MANUFACTURING CO.

MRS. G. BUTTS.

Dissolve 1 pound Spanish whiting in water, stir it thoroughly, and let it settle, then pour off the top, so the grit will be freed. Let the residue settle again, and pour off the top, thus obtaining the pure

Miscellaneous.

whiting; add 1 ounce of borax, dissolved in as little water as necessary; add ½ pint spirits of camphor, 1 pint aqua ammonia. Put in a bottle and cork tight.

SWEET POTATOES KEEP WELL IN SAND.

SWEEP CARPETS with saw dust, wet with borax and ammonia water. There is nothing that freshens up a carpet like this for you have to sweep so hard to get out the saw dust that you clean your carpet well.

TO PRESERVE EGGS FOR WINTER USE.

MRS. GEORGE DANA.

One gallon cold water, 1 pint coarse salt, not quite 1 pint unslacked lime. Mix all together in a stone jar and let it stand 24 hours. It is then ready for the eggs, which may all be put in at once, or from time to time.

ANOTHER WAY TO PRESERVE EGGS FOR WINTER USE.

Grease the surface of the egg thoroughly with a piece of bacon rind. Pack in salt, taking care that the eggs do not touch each other, or the sides of the jar. Always put the small end down.

TO CLEAN MARBLE.

Two parts washing soda, 1 part pumice stone, 1 part finely powdered chalk. Sift through a fine sieve and mix with water. Rub the slab well with this and then wash with soap and water.

TO WASH BLANKETS.

MRS. C. W. ROLSTON.

One bar kitchen soap cut and dissolved in hot water, 2 tablespoons powdered borax. Fold blankets and soak over night or several hours. Do not rub unless there are spots. Squeeze and douse and pull from one hand into the other. Rinse in two or three lukewarm waters and hang in a hot sun without wringing.

Potato water made from boiling 12 or 15 potatoes in 6 quarts of water, pare and slice the potatoes, boil and strain through a hair sieve, when cool enough use it to wash calicoes without soap.

Bran water is good to prevent fading.

Alum will restore green. Dissolve alum one-half the size of an egg in a bucket of water.

Clean zinc with kerosene oil.

Clean copper with turpentine and fine brick dust. Soda is also good, sprinkle on and cover with a wet cloth.

Whites of eggs for burns; also dry flour.

Hot water prevents discoloration from bruises; use it hot as can be borne.

Hot mush will remove pain; it can be used in place of hot fomentations. Spread thick like a mustard plaster. Will keep warm for hours.

HOW TO KEEP AWAY "FLY TIME."

In April and May when the flies seek the sunny window panes kill them then and there. This must be repeated every day. Those large torpid flies will lay thousands of eggs which will be flies by the last of April. Kill them all winter, they often come out with the warm days. Don't let one escape out.

CEMENT FOR FRUIT JARS.

One pound of resin, 2 ounces of mutton tallow, 2 ounces of beeswax. Melt it together.

TO CURE A FELON.

Put your finger in a bag of salt.—H. FEARING.

TO KEEP OFF FLIES.

Sponge the pictures with onion water. This will not injure gilt, wood or glass, and will prevent flies from settling.

WASH matting with salt and water to keep it from turning brown.

WASH oil-cloths with milk and water.

To take fruit stains out of cotton or linen, pour boiling hot water through the stain before washing.

To get rid of rats pulverize copperas and sprinkle it in their holes and wherever they are troublesome.

Oil marks on wall-paper, or the marks where inconsiderate people rest their heads, are a sore grief to good housekeepers, but they can be removed without much trouble. Take pipe-clay or fuller's-earth, and make into a paste, about as thick as rich cream, with cold water; lay it on the stain gently, without rubbing it in; leave it on all night. It will be dry by morning, when it can be brushed off, and unless an old stain, the grease spot will have disappeared. If old renew the application.

Grease on a carpet, if not of long standing, can be readily disposed of by washing the spot with hot soap-suds and borax—half an ounce of borax to a gallon of water. Use a clean cloth to wash it with, rinse in warm water, and wipe dry.

If *spermaceti* is dropped on any garment or furniture, first carefully scrape off all that can be removed without injury to the material; then lay brown paper over the spot, or a piece of blotting-paper, and put a warm iron on the paper until the oil shows through. Continue to renew the paper and apply the warm iron until the paper shows no more oil.

Spots on furniture, from anything hot, or from alcohol, can be removed by rubbing hard with sweet-oil and turpentine. When the spots disappear, wash in milk-warm soap-suds, dry quickly, and polish by rubbing briskly with chamois-skin.

When *velvet* has been wet and becomes spotted, hold the wrong side over steam, and while damp draw the wrong side quickly over a warm iron. It takes two to do this well—one to hold the bottom of the iron upward, and the second to draw the velvet across it.

Paint, pitch or *tar* can be removed from cloth or wood by rubbing it with turpentine. If the paint has become dry, put a few drops of the turpentine on the spot, and let it stand a short time; then rub the spot, and if all the paint is not removed, repeat the work. When entirely gone, rub off with alcohol.

Paint and *putty* can be taken off glass by wetting the glass several times with a strong solution of soda. Wet the glass often with it till the spots soften and can be washed off, and then polish with alcohol.

Ivory that has been spotted, or has grown yellow, can be made as clear and fresh as new by rubbing with fine sand paper, and then polishing with finely powdered pumice-stone.

Marble can be nicely cleaned in the following manner: pulverize a little bluestone, and mix with four ounces of whiting; add to these four ounces of soft soap and one ounce of soda dissolved in a very little water. Boil this preparation over a slow fire fifteen minutes, stirring all the time. Lay it on the marble while hot, with a clean brush. Let it remain half an hour; then wash off in clean suds, wipe dry, and polish by quick rubbing.

Grease can be removed from stone steps or passages by pouring on it strong soda water boiling hot; then make fuller's-earth into a thin paste with boiling water; spread it over the stain or spot, and let it remain all night. If the grease has soaked and dried in, it may be necessary to repeat this for two or three nights, scrubbing it off each morning with strong soap-suds and lye. When houses are under repair and being painted, it is important that one should keep watch for such oil spots, as painters are not overcareful in handling their oils, and such spots are very annoying.

If *ink* has been spilled over rose-wood or mahogany furniture, half a teaspoonful of oil of vitrol in a tablespoonful of water, applied with a feather, will quickly remove it.

A CARPET can be mended by cutting a piece like the carpet a little larger than the hole. Put paste around the edge of the patch, then slip it under the carpet and rub it well with a warm iron until dry. If the figure be matched it makes a very neat job, as well as a quick one.

IT IS said if feather beds and pillows be left out in a drenching rain every spring and afterward exposed to the sun and air on every side until dry, they will be much freshened and lightened.

WASHING RECIPE.

Ten pints of water, 1 pound of soap, shaved finely so as to form a thick soap suds, to this add 2½ tablespoons of kerosene—if you find any oil on the top add more soap. To every gallon of water add 1 pint of this solution.

WASHING RECIPE No. 2.

CLARA DEVERIS.

Ten gallons water, 1 pound soap, cut fine, 2½ tablespoons kerosene oil. Boil the clothes 10 minutes (or more). Rinse in several waters. Spots should be removed before boiling.

WASHING FLUID.

MISS JULIA BARBER.

Dissolve 1 box of concentrated lye in one quart of water, add to it 2 ounces muriate of ammonia, 2 ounces carbonate of potassa and 3 quarts of water. Keep in a stone jug or jar. Use ½ teacupful in the water in which the clothes are boiled (about 3 pailsfull) after rubbing them through one water.

EMERGENCIES — HOW TO AVOID AND HOW TO MEET THEM.

For Poisons.— Give a tumblerful of sweet oil, cream or milk, or white of egg beat up in water. Then cause vomiting as soon as possible by large draughts—at least a pint of luke-warm water, or mustard and water.

For Cuts.— If the blood is bright and flows in *jets*, apply firm pressure upon the *artery above the cut*, nearer the heart. If the blood comes in a steady stream, apply pressure *just below* the cut. For a *slight* cut let the blood flow for half a minute—then dip in cold water. Draw the edges together with sticking plaster, and keep the part quiet a few days.

Nose Bleed.—May be spontaneous and beneficial, relieving fullness of the head. If accidental or undesirable, it may usually be checked by keeping the head nearly erect, applying ice or cold water to the bridge of the nose and nape of the neck—or snuffing up cold water. The clothing should be loose around the neck.

Precautions in Use of Kerosene.—Burn only the *best oil*—which has been thoroughly *tested.* Lamps should be filled *every* day and never lighted when less than half full. Fill lamps by daylight. If *obliged* to fill a lamp at night, place the light at least a yard off, and not in a currant of air. *Never fill a lighted lamp. Never* pour oil on a fire to kindle it.

For Burn and Scalds.— For *slight* burns dip the part instantly in cold water. For severer scalds immerse the part in strong brine, or sprinkle it quickly with cooking soda, and lay over it a wet cloth. When the skin is destroyed, the air may be safely excluded by either of the following: Sweet oil, collodion, pure gum arabic, linseed oil, whiting and water, chalk and vinegar.

Lightning.— During a thunder-storm keep away from doors and windows. The lower part of the house is safer. Do not seek shelter under a tree. Dash cold water on one who is struck.

To Prevent Sunstroke.—Work slowly ; abstain from liquor ; put a wet covering on the head ; cease to labor as soon as headache or dizziness come on. If a person has a sunstroke place him in the shade; loosen the clothing; apply cold water to the head and chest; when perspiration begins, a little stimulant may be given.

Fainting.—Place the person flat upon the back; allow access of fresh air; sprinkle a little cold water on the face.

Apoplexy.—Keep the person in a sitting posture; loosen neck-clothing. Send for physician at once.

Choking.—Hold the head low and slap the back. Blow forcibly into the ear.

To DISLODGE a bean or other hard substance from the nostril, close the other nostril with the fingers and blow forcibly into the mouth.

REMOVE insects from the ear by tepid water. Never put a hard instrument into the ear.

FOR DUST in the eyes, avoid rubbing; dash water into them. If this fails hold the lids down for a few moments by placing the finger upon the lashes—and roll the eye around.

COOKING HUSBANDS.

A BALTIMORE lady has written a receipt for "cooking husbands so as to make them tender and good." It is as follows: "A good many husbands are spoiled by mismanagement. Some women go about as if their husbands were bladders, and blow them up. Others keep them constantly in hot water, others let them freeze by their carelessness and indifference. Some keep them in a stew by irritating ways and words. Others roast them. Some keep them in pickle all their lives. It cannot be supposed that any husband will be tender and good managed in this way, but they are really delicious when properly treated. In selecting your husband you should not be guided by the silvery appearance, as in buying mackerel, nor by the golden tint, as if you wanted salmon. Be sure to select for yourself, as tastes differ. Do not go to market for him, as the best are always brought to your door. It is far better to have none unless you will patiently learn how to cook for him. A preserving kettle of the finest porcelain is best, but if you have nothing but an earthenware napkin, it will do with care. See that the linen in which you wrap him is nicely washed and mended, with the required number of buttons and strings nicely sewed on. Tie him in the kettle by a strong silk cord called comfort, as the one called duty is apt to be weak. They are apt to fly out of the kettle and be burned and crusty on the edges, since like crab and lobsters, you have to cook them while alive. Make a steady fire out of love, neatness and cheerfulness. Set him as near this as seems to agree with him. If he sputters and fizzes, do not be anxious; some husbands do this till they are quite done. Add a little sugar in the form of what confectioners call kisses, but no vinegar or pepper on any account. A little spice improves them, but it must be used with judgment. Do not stick any sharp instrument into him to see if he is becoming tender. Stir him gently, watch the while lest he lie too flat and close to the kettle and so become useless. You cannot fail to know when he is done. If thus treated you will find him very digestible, agreeing nicely with you and the children, and he will keep as long as you want, unless you become careless and set him in too cold a place."

"I have just received the Price List and Samples of Lundborg's Perfumes, for which I sent the manufacturers fifty cents a few days ago. Everybody says they are the best, and everybody is right. I must get a large bottle of one of the odors the first time I go out."

Lundborg's "Edenia."

LUNDBORG'S RHENISH COLOGNE.

If you cannot obtain **Lundborg's Perfumes and Rhenish Cologne** in your vicinity, send your name and address for Price List to the manufacturers,

YOUNG, LADD & COFFIN,

24 Barclay Street,   NEW YORK.

INDEX.

BREADS, YEASTS, HOT CAKES, ETC.—

Apple Johnny cake	1
Bread	1
" No. 2	1
" No. 3	2
" No. 4	2
Boston brown bread	2
Boston tea cake	2
Light bread	2
Buns	3
Brown bread	3
" " No. 2	3
" " No. 3	3
" " No. 4	3
Boston brown bread	4
" " " No. 2	4
Brown muffins	4
Baking powder biscuit	5
Cracked wheat	5
Crackers	5
Cracker toast	6
Corn muffins	6
Corn bread	6
Corn cakes	6
Corn bread No. 2	7
Drop cakes	7
French toast	7
" " No. 2	7
Fritters	7
French rolls	7
Graham muffins	7
Graham bread	8
Huckleberry cake	8
Haresa	8
Indian bread	8
Light rolls	9
" " No. 2	9

Lapland cake	9
" " No. 2	9
Muffins	9
" No. 2	10
" No. 3	10
" No. 4	10
" No. 5	10
Maryland biscuit	10
Parker house rolls	10
Pocket books	11
Pumpkin bread	11
Popovers	11
" No. 2	11
Potato biscuit	11
Rice cake	12
Rolls	12
Steamed bread	12
Split cake	12
Short cake	12
Sally Lunn	13
" " No. 2	13
" " No. 3	13
Sponge	13
Tea cakes	14
Vineyard corn bread	14
Waffles	6
" No. 2	14
Wafers	14
Yeast	15
" No. 2	15
" No. 3	15
" No. 4	15
" No. 5	15
" No. 6	16

ROASTS, BROILS, MEATPIES AND FISH.—

Broiled steak	17
" " No. 2	17
Broiled chicken	17
Beef roast	17
Brine for beef	18
Braised beef	18
Brine for beef No. 2	18
Codfish balls	18

INDEX.

Codfish and eggs No. 1	18
Codfish and eggs No. 2	19
Codfish dinner	19
Chowder	19
Curing hams	19
" " No. 2	20
" " No. 3	20
Calf's head dinner	20
Fried chicken and mush	21
Fried chicken	21
Stewed chicken and rice	21
Chicken pie	22
Corning beef	22
Dressing for turkey	22
Drawn butter	22
Drippings	23
Flank of beef	23
Mackerel	23
Meat	23
Pickle for beef	24
" " " No. 2	24
Stewed chicken	25
Sausage	25
" No. 2	25
" No. 3	25
Turkey	25
" No. 2	26

Soups.—

Bezique soup	27
Beef soup	27
Bouillon of Beef	27
" " " No. 2	28
" " " No. 3	28
Black bean soup	28
Cherry soup	28
Consomme' soup	28
Clear soup	29
Corn soup	29
Green pea soup	29
Gumbo soup	29
Julienne soup	30
Mock turtle soup	30
" " " No. 2	31

Mock oyster soup 31
Mock bisque soup 31
Oyster soup 31
" " No. 2 32
" " No. 3 32
Potato soup 32
Tomato soup 32
Tapioca 32

VEGETABLES.—

Hints for cooking vegetables 33
Asparagus 34
Boston Baked Beans 34
" " " No. 2 34
Baked corn 35
Escalloped Cabbage 35
Cabbage 35
Corn oysters 35
" " No. 2 35
" " No. 3 36
Corn Fritters 3₉
Cucumbers 36
Egg Plant 36
Maccaroni 36
Escalloped onions 36
Parsnips 37
Peas 37
Peas (French) 37
Peas (Creole) 37
Potatoes (Irish way of cooking) 37
" (Stuffed) 37
Escalloped Sweet Potatoes 37
Saratoga Potatoes 38
Stewed Potatoes 38
Southern Potatoes 38
Plain Pilav 39
To boil Rice 39
Ripe Tomato Dolma 39
Green Tomato Dolma 39
Stewed Tomatos 40
Green stewed Tomatos 40
Escalloped Tomatos 40
Turnips 40

INDEX.

Tomatos (Baked) 41
Rice Croquettes 41

BEVERAGES.—

Coffee (French) 42
Chocolate 42
Coffee (boiled) 42
Mock Cream for Coffee 42
Proportion of Coffee 43
Cherry Shrub 43
Lemonade 43
Domestic Ginger Beer 43
Mead 43
Raspberry Vinegar 44
Tea 44
Black Tea 44
Egg Lemonade 44
Syrups 44

CATSUPS, PICKLES, ETC.

Bordeaux sauce 45
Catsup, cucumber 45
" ripe tomato 45
" " " No. 2 45
" " " No. 3 46
" green tomato 46
" currant 46
" gooseberry 46
Chow-chow 47
" " No. 2 47
Chili sauce 47
Pickles, old receipe 47
Pickled corn 48
" cabbage 48
" cherry 48
" cucumber 49
" " No. 2 49
" " No. 3 49
" chopped 50
" French 50
" green tomato 50
" " " No. 2 50
" " " No. 3 51

Pickle, German 51
" grape 51
" martines 51
" peppers 51
" plums 52
" peach 52
" tomatos 52
" sweet 52
" sweet tomato 52
" Spanish 53
" yellow 53
Spiced currants 53

SALADS, SALAD DRESSINGS, OYSTERS, CROQUETTES, ETC.—

Baked salmon 54
Beef loaf 54
Chicken salad 54
" " No. 2 54
" " No. 3 55
" " No. 4 55
Chicken croquettes 55
" " No. 2 55
Cabbage dressing 56
" " No. 2 56
" " No. 3 56
Cream fish 56
Celery salad 56
Escalloped salmon 56
Ham patties 57
Ham for sandwiches 57
Hot slaw 58
Jellied chicken 57
Lettuce dressing 57
Lobster salad 57
Mint sauce 58
Mayonnaise dressing 58
" " No. 2 58
" " No. 3 59
Oysters stewed 59
Oyster pie 59
" " No. 2 59
" " No. 3 60
" sauce for turkey 60

INDEX.

Oysters fricasseed	60
" pickled	60
Oyster sauce for salmon	60
Oysters on toast	61
Oyster chowder	61
Oysters and potatoes	61
" fried. No. 1	61
" " No. 2	62
" escalloped. No. 1	62
" " No. 2	62
Potatoes in croquettes	62
Pate de Veau	63
Potato salad	63
Potting meats	63
Potted liver	64
Pressed veal	64
" chicken	64
Rice croquettes	64
Russian salad	64
Salad dressing	65
" " No. 2	65
" " No. 3	65
Slaw	66
Salmon salad	66
" " No. 2	66
Sweet bread croquettes	66
" " boiled	66
" " fried	66
" " stewed	67
" " broiled	67
" " for invalids	67
Turbot	67
Veal loaf	68
" " No. 2	68

EGGS, OMELETTES, ETC.—

A delicate way to boil eggs	69
To boil eggs	69
Breaded eggs	69
Egg au plat	69
Omelette	69
" No. 2	70
" No. 3	70
" No. 4	70

To scramble eggs 70
To poach eggs 70
Cheese straws 70
Welch rabbit 71
Cheese fondu 71

CAKES AND ICINGS.—

Angel's Food 72
Almond cake 72
Brides " 72
Black " 73
Bermuda spice cake 73
Bradley's cake 73
Bachelor's Buttons 73
Caramel cake 74
Cream cake 74
" " No. 2 74
" " No. 3 74
Cream sponge cake 75
Cup cake 75
Coffee cake 75
Cocoanut cake 75
Cocoanut cones 76
Crullers 76
Cup cake No. 2 76
Cookies 76
" No. 2 76
" No 3 76
" No. 4 76
" No. 5 77
" No. 6 77
Colorado cream cake 77
Detroit spice cake 77
Doughnuts 77
Doughnuts No. 2 78
" " 3 78
" " 4 78
Election cake 78
Fig layer 78
Fig cake 79
Fruit cake 79
Fruit layer cake 79
Fruit cake No. 2 .... 79.

Fruit Cake No. 3	79
" " " 4	79
" " " 5	80
Ginger bread (soft)	80
" " (hard)	80
" "	80
" "	80
" "	81
Ginger snaps	81
" "	81
" bread	81
" " (Nantasket)	81
Ginger cookies	81
" " No. 2	82
Gold and Silver	82
German bread	82
Grandma Dunn's cake	82
Harvard	82
Hermit cookies	82
Hickory nut	83
Harriet	83
Icing	83
Icing (boiled)	83
" No. 2	83
" " 3	83
" " 4	83
Icing without eggs	84
Icing with cream of tartar	84
Ice cream cake	84
Jumbles	84
" No. 2	84
Lady cake	84
Lemon jelly cake	84
Jumbles No. 3	85
Jelly roll	85
Jam cake	85
Loaf cake	85
" " No. 2	85
" " No. 3	86
" " No. 4	86
Lee cake	86
Loaf cake No. 5	86
Marble	87
Ox eyes	87

Orange cake	87
Pine-apple cake	87
Pound cake	87
" " No. 2	88
Rusk	88
Rose cake	88
Sponge cake	88
" " roll	88
" " No. 2	89
" " " 3	89
" " " 4	89
" " " 5	89
" " (molasses)	89
Spice cake	89
" " No. 2	89
" " " 3	90
" " " 4	90
Seed cake	90
" " No. 2	90
Sand tarts	90
" " No. 2	90
Sunshine cake	90
Mrs. de Steiguer's cake	91
Tea cake	91
" " No. 2	91
" " " 3	91
Mrs. Vinton's cake	91
White "	91
" " No. 2	91
" " " 3	92
" mountain cake	92
" nut "	92
Washington "	92

PUDDINGS AND PUDDING SAUCES.—

An attractive pudding	93
Baked custard	93
Birds nest pudding	93
Baked custard. No. 2	94
Boston sago pudding	94
Brown Betty	94
Baked apples	94
Batter pudding	95
Blackberry pudding	95

INDEX.

Baked dumplings		95
Boiled Custard		95
Bread and butter		95
Cheap pudding		96
Chocolate pudding		96
Corn starch "		96
Crawfordsville "		96
Custard		96
" orange		96
" boiled		96
" pudding		97
Corn starch pudding		98
Delmonicos "		98
Eves "		98
Fruit "		98
" " No. 2		99
Fig "		99
Flour "		99
Floating Island		99
" " No. 2		99
Fruit pudding. No. 3		99
Flour "		100
Gold and silver pudding		100
Graham flour "		100
Gelatine "		100
Graham "		100
Hunters "		100
Henrietta's "		100
Indian "	No. 1	101
" "	No. 2	101
" "	No. 3	101
King George's "		101
Pudding sauce		101
" "	No. 2	102
" "	No. 3	102
" "	No. 4	102
" "	No. 5	102
" "	No. 6	102
" "	No. 7	102
" "	No. 8	103
Mrs. Norton's pudding		103
Orange "		103
Orange corn starch pudding		103
Poor man's "		103

Portland corn starch pudding			103
Poor man's	"	No. 2	104
Prune	"		104
Peach	"		104
Rice	"		104
Rice	"	No. 2	105
Suet	"		105
Suet	"	No. 2	105
Snow	"		105
Snow	"	No. 2	105
Sago	"		105
Tapioca	"		106
Tropical snow			106
Mrs. Towne's pudding			106
Tapioca	"	No. 2	106
Tapioca	"	No. 3	106
Taylor	"		107
Thanksgiving	"		107
Yorkshire	"		107

PRESERVES AND JELLIES.—

Apple jelly	108
Cranberry sauce	108
Crab apple preserves	108
Currant jelly	109
Currants preserved	109
Fox grape jelly	109
Orange marmalade	109
Peach preserves	109
Watermelon preserves	110

ICES, CREAMS, JELLIES, ETC.—

Apple ice			111
Amber cream			111
Banana ice cream			112
Bavarian cream			111
Bohemian cream			111
Bevivo			111
Currant ice			112
Charlotte Russe			112
	"	" No. 2	112
	"	" No. 3	112

Charlotte Russe No. 4	113
" " No. 5	113
" " No. 6	113
Chocolate Blanc Mange	114
" " " No. 2	114
Coffee jelly	114
" " No. 2	115
Caramel jelly	114
Coffee cream	114
Corn Starch Blanc Mange and Spanish cream	115
Frozen fruit custard	115
Ice Cream	115
Ice Cream. No. 2	116
Italian cream	116
Iced apples	116
Lemon ice	116
" " No. 2	116
" jelly	117
" " No. 2	117
" " No. 3	117
" cream	117
" butter	117
Macedonian jelly	117
Moonshine	118
Neapolitan Blanc Mange	118
Oakland frozen lemonade	118
Orange jelly	118
Orange sponge	118
Peach Ice Cream	118
Peach jelly	119
Pine-apple jelly	119
Russian cream	119
Scorched cream	119
Tapioca and peaches	119
Tapioca cream	119

PIES, PASTRY, ETC.—

Apple pie	120
Apple minute pie	120
Apple tart	120
Apple pie (chopped)	120
Custard pie	121
Cocoanut pie	121
Chocolate pie	121

Cream pie	121
" " No. 2	122
" " " 3	122
" " " 4	122
" " " 5	122
Lemon pie	122
" " No. 2	123
" " " 3	123
Mince pie. Mrs. Gov. Meigs	123
" " No. 2	123
" " " 3	123
" " " 4	123
Pumpkin pie	124
" " No. 2	124
Potato pie	124
Peach cobbler	124
Puff paste	124
Pie crust	125
Puff paste No. 2	125
" " " 3	125
Pie crust	125
Pie plant pie	125
Peach tart	126
Squash pie	126
Strawberry mountain	126
" short cake	126

CANDIES.—

Amber	127
Butter scotch	127
Cream candy	127
Chocolate caramels	127
" " No. 2	128
English walnuts	128
" " No. 2	128
Cream fig	128
Fruit	128
Lemon	128
Molasses	128
Nut	129
" No. 2	129
Orange bon-bons	129
Pepper mints	129

INDEX.

Taffy	129
White taffy	129
French	130
Honey	130
Hickory nut	130
Vinegar	130
Fig	130
Peanut	131
Hoarhound	131

BUTTER AND CHEESE.—

Butter. No. 1	132
" No. 2	132
" No. 3	133
Cream cheese	133

SICK ROOM.—

Beef tea	134
Cream of tartar beverage	134
Dysentery	134
Disinfectants	135
Flax seed lemonade	135
Gems for dyspeptics	135
Hot milk as a restorative	135
Ingrowing toe-nails	135
Milk and lime water	135
Moss lemonade	136
Oat meal and beef tea	136

MISCELLANEOUS.—

Beef Gall—for washing calicos, carpets, etc	137
Cement for leather	137
Cleaning fluid	137
Corn starch paste	137
Clear starching and ironing	137
Hair wash	138
Leaking lamps	138
Mixture for washing carpets	138
Silver cleaner	138
Sweeping carpets	139
To preserve eggs for winter use	139
" " " " No. 2	139

To clean marble... 139
To wash blankets... 139
How to keep away "fly time"... 140
Washing receipe.. 142
    "   " No. 2 142
Washing fluid.. 142
Emergencies—how to avoid and how to meet them........... 143
Cooking husbands... 144

PURIFY YOUR BLOOD

Good health depends upon pure blood; therefore, to keep well, purify the blood by taking Hood's Sarsaparilla. This medicine is peculiarly designed to act upon the blood, and through that upon all the organs and tissues of the body. It has a specific action, also, upon the secretions and excretions, and assists nature to expel from the system all humors, impure particles, and effete matter through the lungs, liver, bowels, kidneys, and skin. It effectually aids weak, impaired, and debilitated organs, invigorates the nervous system, tones the digestion, and imparts new life and energy to all the functions of the body. A peculiarity of Hood's Sarsaparilla is that it strengthens and builds up the system while it eradicates disease.

"100 Doses One Dollar," so often told of this peculiar medicine, Hood's Sarsaparilla, is not a catch line only, but is absolutely true of and original with this preparation; and it is as absolutely true that it can honestly be applied only to Hood's Sarsaparilla, which is the very best spring medicine and blood purifier. Now, reader, prove it. Take a bottle home and measure its contents. You will find it to hold 100 teaspoonfuls. Now read the directions, and you will find that the average dose for persons of different ages is less than a teaspoonful. Thus economy and strength are peculiar to Hood's Sarsaparilla.

"Hood's Sarsaparilla has driven the poison from my blood, and though 76, I feel active and strong as at 50." W. H. GROESBECK, Brooklyn, N. Y.

Hood's Sarsaparilla Purifies the Blood

"I wish to say that I had salt rheum on my left arm three years, suffering terribly; it almost disabled me from work. I took three bottles of Hood's Sarsaparilla, and the salt rheum has entirely disappeared." H. M. MILLS, 71 French street, Lowell, Mass.

"Hood's Sarsaparilla has done me a very great deal of good. It has built up my general health, given me a regular appetite, and made me full of new life and energy. The sores on my face with which I have suffered many years are so much better that I feel well paid for taking the medicine." MARY ATKINSON, Summerville, Pa.

"I must say Hood's Sarsaparilla is the best medicine I ever used. Last spring I had no appetite, and the least work I did fatigued me ever so much. I began to take Hood's Sarsaparilla, and soon I felt as if I could do as much in a day as I had formerly done in a week. My appetite is voracious." MRS. M. V. BAYARD, Atlantic City, N. J.

"Hood's Sarsaparilla helps me more than any other medicine I have ever taken for general debility, and I have tried almost everything. Our whole family use it, and I consider it ahead of all other medicines for giving strength." MRS. E. BRENEISER, Mauch Chunk, Pa.

Makes the Weak Strong—Creates an Appetite

"I was in bad condition with fainting spells and general debility. I was run down, ate hardly anything, and hardly dared go out on the street alone for fear of having a fainting spell. Hood's Sarsaparilla has done me a wonderful amount of good, as I am now in good health again. My appetite has been good ever since taking the medicine, and I can eat a square meal with relish." MRS. MOLLIE CUTTER, 119 Eleventh street, Covington, O.

Wallace Buck, of North Bloomfield, N. Y., suffered eleven years with a terrible varicose ulcer on his leg, so bad that he had to give up business. He was cured of the ulcer by Hood's Sarsaparilla.

"My wife had dyspepsia. She could not keep her food down, and had that oppressed feeling after eating. She had no appetite, and was tired all the time. She tried numerous medicines without being relieved, but the first bottle of Hood's Sarsaparilla did her a great deal of good. She has now taken two bottles, and can eat anything she wants without having that distress, and has no trouble in retaining her food." JOHN BATTENFIELD, Marion, O.

"Hood's Sarsaparilla as a blood purifier has no equal. It tones the system, strengthens and invigorates, giving new life. I have taken it for kidney complaint, with the best results." D. R. SAUNDERS, 81 Pearl Street, Cincinnati, O.

BE SURE TO GET
Hood's Sarsaparilla

Sold by all druggists. $1; six for $5. Prepared by C. I. HOOD & CO., Lowell, Mass.

Sold by all druggists. $1; six for $5. Prepared by C. I. HOOD & CO., Lowell, Mass.

100 Doses One Dollar   100 Doses One Dollar

PIONEER HOUSES:

A. T. NYE & SON, NYE HARDWARE CO.,
STOVE FOUNDERS, MERCHANTS,
ESTABLISHED A. D. 1828. ESTABLISHED A. D. 1848.

TO SECURE THE BEST RESULTS

FROM THE RECIPES FURNISHED IN THIS BOOK, YOU SHOULD
BUY AT ONCE ONE OF

NYE'S LEADER
COOKING STOVES

MADE IN A LARGE VARIETY OF STYLES, PATTERNS AND SIZES.

ALWAYS RELIABLE, HOME MADE,
HANDSOMEST AND BEST.

Nye Hardware Co.,

GENERAL HARDWARE DEALERS,

NOS. 10 AND 12 FRONT STREET,

MARIETTA, OHIO.

Blackmore & Kinsey,

—— DEALERS IN ——

PROVISIONS

—— AND COVERS OF ——

"BUCKEYE"

AND

"SILVER STAR"

BRANDS OF

HAMS!

38 & 40 Vine Street,

CINCINNATI.

LADIES!

IF YOU WILL WEAR A NICE FITTING, COMFORTABLE PAIR OF

SHOES

DURING THE PREPARATION OF THESE DISHES, YOU WILL BE MORE CERTAIN OF SUCCESS THAN IF TORMENTED BY AN ILL-SHAPED SHOE. THE FORMER YOU WILL BE MORE LIKELY TO OBTAIN OF

THE H. LORD SHOE CO.

THAN ELSEWHERE BY REASON OF THE LARGER ASSORTMENT THERE OFFERED. WHEN IN NEED OF FOOTWEAR STOP AT

57 FRONT STREET, MARIETTA, OHIO,

AND GET A FIT.

MILLINERY.

MRS. S. BURLINGAME

KEEPS A FULL LINE OF MILLINERY CONSTANTLY ON HAND. PATTERN HATS AND BONNETS A SPECIALTY.

59 Front St. Marietta, O.

WHEN USING RECEIPTS IN THIS BOOK REMEMBER TO GET

Styer's Flavors, Spices and Baking Powder

MADE ONLY BY W. H. STYER, THE LEADING DRUGGIST, MARIETTA, O.

Our Laundry Starch

Is the Best Ever Offered the Public.

No Housekeeper

Should Allow her Laundress to Get an Inferior Article.

Our Corn Starch

FOR FOOD is Perfectly Pure and Thoroughly Sweet.

Never Take Starch

Unless it Bears the Name of

The George Fox Starch Co.

Cincinnati, O.

NEAL'S ✢ CARRIAGE ✢ PAINTS.

SEVEN BEAUTIFUL SHADES.

Brilliant, Simple, Durable and Economical.

The Original and Only Complete Line of
Liquid Carriage Paint ever Introduced.

BEWARE OF WORTHLESS IMITATIONS.

☞ Just the thing for repairing old Buggies and Wagons. Experience not necessary to apply. One coat for old work. VARNISHING UNNECESSARY. Dries perfectly hard, with a beautiful gloss. An old buggy can be repainted at a cost, NOT TO EXCEED ONE DOLLAR. The MERITS of the MATERIALS USED, and our SPECIAL MANUFACTURING FACILITIES, enables us to present a CARRIAGE PAINT which is absolutely unsurpassed, while the simplicity of application and the beauty of appearance will be manifest at once.

ACME WHITE LEAD & COLOR WORKS, Sole Manufacturers, DETROIT, MICH.

For Sale by W. H. Buell & Co., Marietta, O.

GATES & PAYNE,

Seedsmen

AND GENERAL MERCHANTS,

No. 11 Front Street,

MARIETTA OHIO.

GOOD HOUSEKEEPERS USE **DWIGHT'S** COW BRAND **SODA**

SOLD EVERYWHERE. BUY IT.

The Akron Cracker Co.

AKKON, OHIO,

MANUFACTURERS OF SUPERIOR BRANDS OF

CRACKERS,

CAKES AND BISCUITS.

THESE GOODS ALWAYS FRESH ARE KEPT IN STOCK BY

BOSWORTH, WELLS & CO.,

MARIETTA, OHIO.

C. T. BUTLER.   J. E. VANDERVOORT.

BUTLER & VANDERVOORT.

Dry Goods Retailers and Jobbers.

47 FRONT ST., MARIETTA, O.

N. B. We spare no pains to secure for our customers the best *fabrics*, both Foreign and Domestic, and aim to offer the most thoroughly reliable goods at the most attractive prices. We make a specialty of Black Silks and ask a comparison of qualities and prices with goods offered anywhere in this country. We shall be pleased to send samples by mail on application.

BUTLER & VANDERVOORT,
General Dry Goods Dealers.   MARIETTA, OHIO.

DUTCHER'S READY CLEANER.

AN INDISPENSIBLE REQUISITE!

Removes Grease, Oil, Paint, Stains, Dirt from Clothing, Hats, Carpets, Dress Goods, Soiled Hands, Laces, Fine Fabrics, and Cleans Hats, Coats, Vests, Pants, Dress Goods and Woolen Fabrics Quick.

NO ODOR. Articles cleansed may be used at once. Renders soiled hands clean and soft. Removes the odor of perspiration, leaving the skin refreshed, enlivened and clean. Once used it will be added to the list of

HOME COMFORTS.

Mrs. F. says: — I removed the grease from hot lard spilled upon my cashmere dress, with the first application of Ready Cleaner. Using it freely I dissolved the grease, then rinsed with cold water.

Mrs. C.—A large kerosene lamp fell to the floor and scattered its contents upon the carpet. Ready Cleaner took out all the grease without injury to color or fabric.

Mrs. L.—I have used Ready Cleaner to remove soiled spots in my carpets and clothing. It is a success in every place.

H. E. L. — A few strokes of the sponge, wet with Ready Cleaner removed gearing grease from my overcoat.

A lady in Brandon, Vt., says: — My son spilled kerosene on his clothes from head to foot. I supposed the suit was ruined. I used Dutcher's Ready Cleaner and soon removed every particle of grease. After pressing, the suit was as good as before.

ECONOMY.

Use Dutcher's Ready Cleaner. Clean up the old hats, coats, vests, pants, dresses, outside garments; press them over, mend them up and they will answer for another six months. It costs but 25 cents.

Mechanics, Artisans, and those whose occupations necessitate soiled hands, will find in the Ready Cleaner an article that will at once render their hands clean and soft. Ask your druggist to order it.

In large bottles 25 cents. For sale by the trade generally.

FREDERICK DUTCHER & SONS, Prop'rs, St. Albans, Vt.

Baron & King,
Artistic ✢ ✢
✢ Photographers

New Styles, New Accessories, New Designs.

₊ The Very Finest Work at Reasonable Prices.

Successors to J. D. Cadwallader. Come and See us.

T. W. Moore.   F. M. Reed.

T. W. Moore & Co.,
General ✢ ✢
✢ Merchandise

Grain, Feed, Salt, Produce and Flour.

Always on Hand, Shingles, Glass, Nails, Lime.

Harmar, Ohio.

SHOCKING ACCIDENT
AND
WONDERFUL CURE.

[*From the New York Daily Times, July 3, 1885*]

Shocking Accident and Wonderful Cure.

An occurrence so remarkable in its results that they would not be believed if not fully attested has recently taken place here. A boy named John H. Malkmus, employed in the soap and perfumery works of Mr. Solon Palmer, Nos. 374 and 376 Pearl Street, took hold of a dull red hot iron. His right hand was terribly burned, and he suffered excruciating torture. Palmer's Lotion was promptly applied, the bandages being kept well saturated with it. In an hour the pain was almost gone. In five days the hand was well, and not a scar remained. The boy made an affidavit that the marvelous cure had been effected solely by the use of Palmer's Lotion.

PALMER'S LOTION IS EQUALLY EFFICACIOUS IN THE CURE OF

QUINSY SORE THROAT,	PIMPLES,	RINGWORM,
PUTRID SORE THROAT,	TETTER,	BARBER'S ITCH,
CANKER IN THE MOUTH,	ECZEMA,	PILES,
SORE EYES.	BRUISES,	SALT RHEUM.	CHILBLAINS,

And every other disease of the skin or mucous membranes that can be reached by an external application. It is kept in every workshop, kitchen and bedroom wherever its marvelous healing properties are known.

PALMER'S LOTION SOAP

possesses all the valuable properties of the Lotion, but in a milder form. It is the great Skin and Complexion Soap,
For full particulars, see large circular.

PREPARED ONLY BY

SOLON PALMER,
374 & 376 Pearl St.   NEW YORK.

For Sale by Druggists Generally.

Granite Floor Paint.

You have undoubtedly in your experience, had occasion to paint a floor, steps or piazza.

If such is the case, the chances are that you realize that the same paint used for painting the exterior of houses will not answer to paint floors, yet up to the time we invented the GRANITE FLOOR PAINT that was what must be used.

There are three great faults with the paints heretofore used, namely: First, they require a long time to dry, which causes great inconvenience; second, they never dry perfectly hard, and consequently will not wear; third, cold water will stain, hot water blister, and soap will to a certain extent remove them.

After many long and costly experiments we succeeded in perfecting the GRANITE FLOOR PAINT, and present it to the public with the assurance that it has none of the above faults.

It is sure to become as great a favorite as our other popular specialty, *Neal's Carriage Paint*, which is prepared ready for use in eight beautiful colors, and renders the re-painting of a buggy possible at a cost of not to exceed one dollar.

ACME WHITE LEAD & COLOR WORKS,
SOLE MANUFACTURERS,
DETROIT, MICHIGAN.
For sale by W. H. BUELL & CO., MARIETTA, OHIO.

J. H. DYE & SONS,
LIVERY, SALE AND FEED
STABLES,

No. 41 North Third Street,

MARIETTA, OHIO.

WE invite the attention of all good housekeepers to the merits of THE J. MONROE TAYLOR GOLD MEDAL SALERATUS AND SODA, as superior in quality, more healthy, and to produce whiter and lighter bread foods of all kinds, and to take a little less to do the work.

These goods are manufactured with special regard to their healthfulness by an improved chemical and mechanical process, and not in use by any other manufacturer of soda or saleratus.

By these processes the alkalies are three times refined, the carbonic acid thoroughly washed and filtered, thus eliminating all sulphates and impurities (which are left in many inferior brands) rendering the Gold Medal absolutely of the highest degree of purity, and so justly celebrated wherever introduced.

The Gold Medal Saleratus or Soda, which are one and the same thing, if properly used with sour milk or buttermilk, or pure cream tartar, will be found much cheaper, more healthy, and superior to the best brands of baking powders, to say nothing of the many cheap brands, which are inferior, injurious, detrimental to health, and should be avoided.

E. R. DURKEE & CO'S
SELECT SPECIALTIES

SPICES & MUSTARD

SOLD ONLY IN FULL-WEIGHT SEALED PACKAGES.

Guaranteed absolutely pure. Some manufacturers use the word PURE as a decoy. Consumers would do well to remember that an article may be pure, but lack other essential qualities. Our Select Spices are warranted uniform in quality, and to excel all others in strength, richness, flavor and cleanliness.

SALAD DRESSING
AND
COLD MEAT SAUCE.
THE ORIGINAL AND ONLY GENUINE.
WITHOUT A RIVAL AS A DRESSING FOR ALL SALADS, AND AS A SAUCE FOR COLD MEATS, ETC.

It is prepared with extreme care; all its ingredients are of the PUREST and BEST, and will keep good for years.

We warn consumers against all mixtures put up in imitation of our style of package.

CHALLENGE SAUCE,
For ROAST BEEF, CHOPS, SOUPS, GRAVIES, FISH, Etc.
A STRICTLY FIRST-CLASS TABLE SAUCE.

Pleases the taste; promotes digestion; stimulates the appetite.

Connoisseurs have pronounced it THE ONLY REALLY GOOD AMERICAN SAUCE, and in many respects greatly superior to any imported.

CELERY SALT.
STRONGER IN FLAVOR THAN THE PLANT ITSELF. PUT UP IN ATTRACTIVE STYLE. FOR TABLE USE.

THESE GOODS ARE SOLD BY ALL DEALERS IN FINE GROCERIES, AND ARE WARRANTED TO GIVE FULL SATISFACTION.

GEORGE DANA & SON,

BELPRE, OHIO.

PRODUCERS OF

PURE CIDER VINEGAR,

EXPORATED FRUITS

AND PACKERS OF

HERMETICALLY SEALED FRUITS

AND

VEGETABLES.

ALL GOODS OF EXTRA QUALITY

AND GUARANTEED TO BE ABSOLUTELY PURE.

DANA FARM,

Settled 1789.   BELPRE, O.

Cholera Cramps Colic

all Summer Complaints and all Bowel Troubles are cured by

Perry Davis' Pain Killer

All druggists sell it.

M. SEIPEL & CO.,
ARE HEADQUARTERS FOR

FANCY GOODS AND NOTIONS
ALSO KEEP A FULL LINE OF

DRY GOODS AND
GENTS' FURNISHING GOODS.

A Large Assorted Stock at Lowest Prices.

AGENTS FOR THE CELEBRATED DAVIS SEWING MACHINES.

No. 61 FRONT STREET,
MARIETTA, OHIO.

G. L. SPENCE,
THE ONLY
MUSIC ❖ AND ❖ ART ❖ STORE
IN MARIETTA.

DECKER BROS., J. & C. FISCHER, HAINES BROS.,
AND OTHER FIRST-CLASS PIANOS,
AND THE WORLD-FAMED ESTEY ORGAN,
ALL SELL ON EASY PAYMENTS.
LARGE STOCK OF PICTURES,
ALL KINDS, GRADES AND PRICES,
CABINET FRAMES AND ALBUMS.
EASELS, LARGE AND SMALL,
WALL POCKETS AND FANCY GOODS
FOR XMAS, BIRTHDAY AND
WEDDING PRESENTS.
SEVERAL DIFFERENT MAKES OF SEWING MACHINES
SOLD AT ROCK BOTTOM PRICES.
TUNING AND REPAIRING PIANOS AND ORGANS.
REPAIRING SEWING MACHINES,
NEEDLES, OIL, AND PARTS AT

G. L. SPENCE, NEAR COURT HOUSE.

The L. & M. Pure Prepared Paints sold only by W. H. Buell & Co., Marietta, O., covers over 250 square feet two coats, at a cost for material not exceeding $1.25. Estimate the cost of painting your dwelling upon this basis. Every package bears the following guarantee: "Any building that is not satisfactorily painted with our paint, or upon which its use has not cost less than if other paints had been used, will be re-painted at our expense."

Yours truly,

Longman & Martinez.

www.ingramcontent.com/pod-product-compliance
Lightning Source LLC
Chambersburg PA
CBHW031828230426
43669CB00009B/1262